Wild Boar

Animal

Series editor: Jonathan Burt

Wild Boar

Dorothy Yamamoto

REAKTION BOOKS

For Mike

Published by
REAKTION BOOKS LTD
Unit 32, Waterside
44–48 Wharf Road
London N1 7UX, UK
www.reaktionbooks.co.uk

First published 2017
Copyright © Dorothy Yamamoto 2017

Printed and bound in China

A catalogue record for this book is available from the British Library

ISBN 978 1 78023 761 9

Contents

1 What is a Wild Boar?

According to the *Oxford English Dictionary*, 'wild boar' is the 'usual name of the wild species (*Sus scrofa*) found in the forests of Europe, Asia, and Africa'. As such, wild boar are the ancestors of domestic pigs (subspecies *Sus scrofa domesticus*). If one could draw a straightforward line of descent, from wild forebear to farmed animal, things would be simple. But they are not.

In his book *Pig* (2011), Brett Mizelle describes the process of domestication and the accompanying changes in the animals' appearance. The spots and stripes that had helped wild pigs blend into their surroundings vanished, tails curled, and ears, previously pricked for danger, flopped. The bodies of domesticated pigs became longer, and their legs shorter.[1] Of course, these changes took a considerable time, and many of the pigs in medieval manuscript illustrations look more like our idea of wild boars, with narrow snouts, alert ears and slender, bristled bodies with a crest of hair running along the spine. Animals like these appear, for instance, in the Queen Mary Psalter (*c.* 1310–20), feeding under oak trees on the acorns which swineherds are knocking down from the branches. The Luttrell Psalter, prepared for Sir Geoffrey Luttrell of Irnham in Lincolnshire in the early fourteenth century, shows a similar scene; the Psalter also has a separate vignette of a tusked boar with a curly tail.[2] The practice of pannage – letting pigs loose in woodland, to forage for their own food – would

Pigs feeding on acorns; detail from the early 14th-century Luttrell Psalter.

certainly have meant that the wild boar had opportunities to mate with the farmed herd, especially as the acorn harvest coincided with the time of their rut. Indeed, the word 'hybrid', although not in general use until the seventeenth century, derives from the Latin *hibrida*, which specifically denoted the offspring of a tame sow and a wild boar. Even today, many breeds of pigs, from the hairy-coated Duroc to the Tamworth, with its pricked ears and long snout, differ in appearance from the familiar smooth pink pig of children's stories.

Wild boar, from the early 14th-century Luttrell Psalter.

'Wild boar', therefore, is a cultural as much as a biological descriptor. In 1842, in his *Breeds of the Domestic Animals of the British Islands*, David Low prefaces his chapter on the 'Wild Hog' with a picture of a 'Wild Boar and Sow, imported from Alentejo in Portugal, and presented to the Earl of Leicester by his Royal Highness the Duke of Sussex'. Although the pair are hairy, their drooping ears and general body shape, together with the sow's curly tail, show that they are not true-bred animals but crosses with domestic stock. Yet their value undoubtedly lay in the 'wild' label that had been attached to them.

In fact most of the wild boar in Europe today have a genetic make-up that includes material from domestic pigs. This is especially the case where a population has been reintroduced – either accidentally or on purpose – after becoming extinct in its homeland. For example, genetic sampling of the boar now living in the Forest of Dean, on the border between England and Wales, has shown that they are of mixed ancestry, some even bearing an allele exclusive to Japanese wild boar (presumably the product of

WILD BOAR & SOW.

some interchange between breeders in the last century).[3] Does this really matter? In their set of guidelines for reintroduction of a formerly native species, the World Conservation Union recommend that the source population used should ideally be closely related genetically to the original stock. So opponents of the continued presence of boar in the Forest of Dean could argue that they are not a true native species brought back from the brink, but feral escapees with an entirely different pedigree. On the other hand, they certainly look like wild boar, and, as author Martin Goulding robustly argues, 'A useful working definition is that *if it looks like a wild boar, acts like a wild boar, and fills the ecological niche of a wild boar, then it is a wild boar.*'[4]

If we picture a wild boar, we see a fierce, sharp-tusked, hairy beast, very different from a farmyard pig. But there is an equally wide gulf in our attitudes towards these two animals. As pigs have come more completely under human control, so wild boar have moved beyond it, and have become larger, wilder and more ferocious in our imagination. This inflation of threat runs through the history of their interaction with humans, springing from the earliest encounters, when they presented both an opportunity and a danger: a valuable food source, but also a formidable foe with tusks that could inflict terrible injuries. The boar's deadly impact upon human bodies is a running theme in legends, stories and reports about it, and fighting and killing one single-handededly was the mark of a great warrior. Now that the hunters are no longer armed with boar-spears but with high-velocity rifles, the boars have ballooned into monstrous hybrids such as the American 'Hogzilla', in order to maintain the theme of heroic combat. Where people previously unfamiliar with wild boar are coming into contact with them – perhaps because the boar have extended their range, as in Berlin, or, in the Forest of Dean, because a population has been newly introduced – there are often distorted perceptions of their size and behaviour.

A boar hunt decorates the side of a pietra dura casket from Florence, now at Charlecote Park, Warwickshire, England.

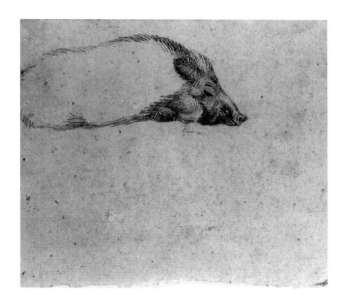

Yet wild boar are usually only aggressive towards humans if surprised or provoked. They are generally active at dusk or at night-time, making accidental encounters less likely. It is their misfortune that their history bears so heavily upon our view of them.

2 The Natural Boar

Wild boar have the widest natural range of any ungulate (hoofed mammal) in the world. They can live in a variety of habitats, provided they have bushy cover so they can shelter from predators, and water to drink and bathe in. They do not cope well in snow, which impedes their movements and makes them much more vulnerable to attack by wolves. However, a series of milder, less snowy winters in Finland in the 1980s marked a spread of wild boar northwards, and it can be expected that future climate change due to global warming will allow similar extensions of their range.[1]

In Europe, boar prefer deciduous and mixed forests, ideally with boggy areas, as they do not have sweat glands and so need to wallow to prevent overheating. The Białowieża Forest in Poland, where they are particularly numerous, is an ideal habitat. However, they can also occupy alpine zones, and live at heights of up to 4,000 metres (13,000 ft) in the mountains of Central Asia and Kazakhstan. In conifer forests the boar use their tusks to rip away pieces of bark, releasing the pine resin. They rub themselves against the tree to transfer the resin to their coats, where it acts to repel insects and parasites. It also hardens 'like lacquer', according to Japanese hunters, who thought the boar did this deliberately so that their coats would deflect arrows.[2]

It is debatable how many subspecies of wild boar there are – estimates range from sixteen to 25 – but four regional groupings

European wild boar in its wallow.

are generally recognized: Western, Indian, Eastern and Indonesian. These differ in such characteristics as size, shape of the skull and prominence of the spinal crest or 'mane'. While all have a coat of short, thick, bristly hair, its colour ranges from brown to black to grey, according to subspecies and location. (For instance, Western European boar generally have brown coats, while those in Eastern Europe are blacker – a distinction which could once be seen in the animals from different regions imported into Britain.) Along the boar's spine grows an upright line of longer hair, which has given rise to its common name of 'razorback' in the southern United States. In the future some subspecies may come to lose their distinctive identity – as an example, the

Winifred Austin, 'Indian Wild Boar', plate from Frank Finn, *The Wild Beasts of the World* (1909).

genetic purity of *S. scrofa riukiuanus*, found only on the Ryukyu Islands of Japan, is threatened by hunters who bring larger boar over from the mainland, so that they will interbreed and increase the size of the native animals, thus providing better sport.

Wild boar are well engineered to succeed and prosper in a multiplicity of habitats. The whole weight and force of the body is loaded forwards: the area behind the shoulder blades rises into a hump, while the neck is short and inflexible. The massive head accounts for up to one-third of the body's length. The snout ends in a cartilaginous disc supported by a small bone called the prenasal, and this allows the animal to bulldoze its way into compacted or frozen ground with ease and turn over rocks of up to 50 kilograms (110 lb). Wild boar can run at a speed approaching

COARSE WORK
THE PUP: I call that very poor dentistry.

'Coarse Work',
wood engraving
by 'Anderson',
undated.

40 km/h (24 mp/h) and leap up to 1.5 metres (5 ft), and are also excellent swimmers. All males display prominent canine teeth, or tusks. These develop when the animal is two years old, and grow throughout its life; the lower canines, its most formidable weapon, are sharpened by being honed against the upper ones.

European wild boar in the Forest of Dean, England.

Like all other even-toed ungulates, wild boar have cloven hooves, formed of two main toes, encased in a layer of horn, with a smaller toe on the outside of each of these. An original fifth toe has been lost through evolution. The toes can spread, making it easier for the boar to walk on soft ground.

It has recently been discovered that wild boar (together with warthogs and many other creatures, including birds, ruminants, dogs and woodmice) have an internal compass which allows them to orient themselves using the earth's magnetic field. The study, which was carried out on animals in the Czech Republic, found that the boar strongly preferred to line up their nests along a north–south axis. The researchers speculate that 'a magnetic sense would, for example, help boars put several feeding grounds into global perspective, therefore facilitating quick switching between them when needed.' The scientists also warn that nearby electric power lines may disrupt this sense, causing the boar to become disoriented, with a possible human cost in an increasing number of collisions as the animals wander across roads.[3]

Wild boar have poor eyesight and among the primary colours can only distinguish blue. However, this is not a great handicap, since blue is the colour most easily seen in the low light conditions – dusk and night-time – in which the boar are generally active. Their sense of smell is acute, and so is their hearing. As social animals, they communicate with a range of vocalizations – rumbling when content, squealing when injured, or snorting through

A wild boar family relax in the forest.

18

the nose when disturbed or frightened. When courting a female the male will try to rest his chin on her rump while grunting rhythmically in what is known as the mating chant.

It is not surprising that wild boar have few predators apart from humans: their main threats come from wolves, and from leopards, tigers and crocodiles in the eastern part of their range. Wolves do not usually tackle a fully grown animal, but they may have a devastating effect on a local population by targeting piglets and adolescents. Wild boar, however, can also benefit from sharing their habitat with predators, since they will scavenge leftover carrion, and may even drive smaller predators, such as lynx, away so they can feed on the kill themselves.

In fact, wild boars' chances for survival are enhanced by their opportunistic omnivorousness – they will eat practically anything. (Japanese hunters call the boar *yama no sōjiya*, 'the cleaner of the mountain'.) Most of their diet is made up of plant matter, such as leaves, berries, grasses, fruits, nuts such as acorns, and roots and bulbs unearthed by their snouts, but they will also take eggs, worms, small reptiles such as lizards, small rodents and the young of ground-nesting birds. Those living near the Volga delta feed on carp, roach and molluscs, as well as cormorant and heron chicks, and in the Forest of Dean in England they have been seen eating frogs. Although wild boar have become a byword for messy eating and gluttony, those in Basel Zoo have been observed carrying their food – apples, beetroot or pieces of meat – to a stream in order to wash it.[4] In the wild, boar do most of their foraging at night. During daylight hours they rest up in 'day nests' – depressions in the ground that are sometimes lined with leaves or vegetation.

A group of wild boar is called a 'sounder' and will typically consist of two or three adult females and their young. Outside the mating season, full-grown males usually live alone – the words for 'boar' in both French (*sanglier*) and Italian (*cinghiale*) derive from the Latin for 'solitary pig', *singularis porcis*. Their solitary lifestyle, together with the fact that they can grow to a formidable size – up to 200 kilograms (440 lb), with a body length of up to 2 metres (6.5 ft) – has primed them to be the target of human hunters in many societies. Their reputation for ferocity has been heightened by the froth that appears at their mouth as they clash their tusks together – although this is not to signal aggression but to secrete a pheromone which attracts females by showing they are ready to breed.

Males are sexually mature at ten months, but will not be able to compete successfully for females until they are fully grown, at about five years of age. (In the wild, provided they have not been intensively hunted, the average lifespan of a boar is about ten years, although in captivity they have been known to live for nearly thirty.) Females are able to bear young from eighteen months, and usually come into oestrus in the autumn, in October and November. It is then that males battle each other for the right to breed, and the injuries they sustain can sometimes be fatal. As a compensatory adaptation, they have developed thickened tissue around their chests and necks, which becomes even thicker during the rut to provide protection against an opponent's stabbing tusks.

Wild boar piglets are born in the spring. A couple of days before she is due to give birth, the sow leaves the sounder and builds a farrowing nest out of vegetation, above a hollow scrape lined with twigs. Litters generally consist of four to six piglets, but can be as large as twelve. The piglets (called 'humbug' in Britain, *marcassin* in France or *uribou*, 'watermelon boy', in Japan) have coats with longitudinal stripes of light brown and cream, the better to blend into the shifting shadows of their forest home. At birth they weigh from 750 grams to 1 kilogram (1.5–2 lb), and

spend their first few days within the nest, pressed together for warmth. They then follow their mother as she rejoins the sounder, and may be communally parented as well as suckle from other sows who have given birth at the same time. They quickly start to root for food, and are weaned at three to four months old.

Wild boar sow with piglet.

Both the range and numbers of wild boar have fluctuated dramatically in recent centuries, due to human activity. Historically, hunting has been a major factor: in Britain, the last wild boar was probably killed in the early modern era; in Sweden the species became extinct in the sixteenth century, and in Denmark in the early 1800s. However from the middle of the twentieth century the animal's range has expanded, and it has recolonized territories (such as large areas of Germany and Italy) from which it had previously been driven. Local populations have been created – or augmented – by escapees from farms, zoos and private collections.

Wild boar in the USA are non-native, the descendants of animals brought in by the conquistadors Hernán Cortés and Hernando de Soto in the sixteenth century, or imported during the nineteenth and twentieth centuries so that they could be hunted for sport. They have proliferated in vast numbers – there are now several million in the USA and Canada – posing both an opportunity and a problem: escapees from farms in the Canadian provinces of Alberta and Saskatchewan multiplied so rapidly in the first decades of the twenty-first century that bounties were offered for pairs of ears.

Wild boar and their behaviour have long been watched and commented on by writers interested in the natural world. The earliest naturalists often mingled direct observation with legends or travellers' tales. So the ancient Roman author Pliny the Elder (*c.* AD 23–79) noted that boars are very dangerous in the breeding

A piglet begins its journey to independence.

season, when they harden their sides by rubbing them against the trunks of trees and coat their backs with dirt by wallowing in mud. He also described the ferocity of the sows in protecting their young. However, he also believed that the wild boar found in India had extra tusks springing from their foreheads, like 'a calf's horns'.[5]

Wild boar were observed with particular diligence because hunting them was such a popular and highly esteemed activity.

Jan Swart van
Groningen,
Gluttony,
16th century.

It made sense for the hunter to find out all he could about his
quarry. Oppian, the author of a second-century AD Greek hunting
treatise, the *Cynegetica*, transfers the fury and passion of the
hunted boar to its iconic tusks:

> There is a tale touching the Wild Boar that his white tusk
> has within it a secret devouring fiery force . . . For when
> a great thronging crowd of hunters with their Dogs lay
> the beast low upon the ground . . . then if one take a thin
> hair from the neck and approach it to the tusk of the still
> gasping beast, straightway the hair takes fire and curls
> up. And on either side of the Dogs themselves, where the

fierce tusks of the Swine's jaws have touched them, marks of burning are traced upon the hide.[6]

Oppian interpreted the foam that the male boar produces as an indicator of its readiness to breed as evidence of its violent and uncontrollable lust:

> Unceasingly he roams in pursuit of the female and is greatly excited by the frenzy of desire . . . He drops foam upon the ground and gnashes the white hedge of his teeth, panting hotly; and there is much more rage about his mating than modesty. If the female abide his advances, she quenches all his rage and lulls to rest his passion. But if she refuses intercourse and flees, straightway stirred by the hot and fiery goad of desire he either overcomes her and mates with her by force or he attacks her with his jaws and lays her dead in the dust.[7]

In the Middle Ages, Christian belief that the world itself was the Word of God, and that every living thing had its own special meaning, produced the moralized compendia known as bestiaries. Here the fighting spirit of the boar was said to signify 'the fierceness of the rulers of this world', while in a transferred sense the animal might represent one of the Seven Deadly Sins (most commonly Anger, Lust or Gluttony) or even the Devil himself. In a bogus etymology first concocted by the seventh-century scholar Isidore of Seville, the boar's Latin name, *aper*, was said to be derived from *feritate*, 'ferocity' (with a 'p' substituted for the 'f'). The thirteenth-century encyclopedist Bartholomaeus Anglicus recycled the well-worn theme of the boar's fierceness and 'cruelty', but added that if the boar feels his tusks are getting blunt, he 'seeketh a herb that is called *origanum*, and gnaweth it and cheweth it, and cleanseth and comforteth the roots of his teeth therewith by virtue thereof.'[8]

Once the boar had been identified with sin, every aspect of its appearance and behaviour could be made to yield up a moral lesson. In the fourteenth-century French hunting manual *Les livres du roy Modus et de la royne Ratio* (The Books of King Method and Queen Reason), Queen Ratio lays into the boar, which she says is black and ugly, like those who have lost the light of the spirit and live in benighted worldliness. The boar shoves its face into the soil, like those whose only concern is filling their bellies and enjoying the delights of the flesh. Even its feet are twisted and crossed, like those of the Devil – a warning to those vain people who favoured the shoes that were then in vogue, with their exaggeratedly pointy toes.[9]

In the early modern period, Edward Topsell (*c.* 1572–1625) noted that the boar's neck was 'broad and thicke, and in it lyeth the strength of the beast'. It has 'a collop [fold of flesh] next to the necke called vulgarly *Callasum*', which should be 'broad and stiffe' in a healthy animal, and a hard ridge on its snout to plough through the soil. Topsell repeated the old story about the boar's insatiable lust, which led it to force itself upon, or kill, a reluctant female, a fury he thought was caused by an excess of seed (sperm): 'Being inflamed with venereal rage, he so setteth upright the bristles of his neck, that you would take them to be the sharp fins of Dolphins; then champeth he with his mouth, grateth and gnasheth his teeth one against another, and breathing forth his boyling spirit, not only at his eyes, but at his foaming white mouth.' The blood of wild boars, Topsell wrote, is 'black like black wine', their tears are 'very sweet', and their urine is so hot that it burns them: 'they can never run away in flight till they have emptied their bellies thereof.' Boars know how to cure themselves of digestive disorders: if they have accidentally eaten

poisonous plants such as hemlock or henbane, 'they crawl to the water sides, where they gather together Snails and Sea-crabs, by eating whereof they are restored to their former health.' Topsell includes a list of the various 'epithets' of the boar, adding up to a composite portrait:

> sharp, wilde . . . bloudy, toothered, hard . . . cruell, outrageous, fierce, strong, gnashing, lightning, yellow, raging, Acorn-gatherer, quick, rough, rough-haired, horrible . . . threatning, woodwanderer . . . bristle-bearer, foaming, strict, filthy . . . fearful, wry-faced, truculent, devourer, violent . . . wound-maker, impetuous, mountain-liver, armed on both sides, and such like.[10]

The great French naturalist Georges-Louis Leclerc, Comte de Buffon (1707–1788), considered the boar in the fifth volume of his massive *Histoire naturelle*, in a chapter entitled 'The Swine, the Hog of Siam, and the Wild Boar'. Buffon found the species

Das Wildschwein.
Sus scrofa aper, fem.

puzzlingly anomalous and was uncertain whether it should be
classed with 'whole-hoofed', 'cloven-hoofed' or 'digitated' animals,
since hogs have four toes yet walk on only two of them. In addition, they produce so many young that they 'even [seem] to form
the extremity of the viviparous species and approach the ovipar-
ous'. Buffon was bothered by the hog's 'ambiguous' nature – those
redundant toes and swarms of piglets – but concluded that there
must be some species that 'fill up the intervals' in Nature's overall
design, and that Nature herself operates on a far grander and
more complex scale than we can imagine.

In general, Buffon considered hogs, both wild and domesticated, to be coarse, brutal and incorrigibly gluttonous. Just as
Nature might appear to have bodged their design, so their entire
behaviour is rough and uncouth. Their sense of touch is so dull
that 'Mice have been known to lodge on their backs, and to eat
their skin and fat without their seeming sensible of it.' Wild boar

28

will eat anything and everything: as well as wild fruits, worms and roots, they will devour carrion, and 'the skin of the deer, and the claws of birds have been found in their stomach'. Unfairly, Buffon attributed the co-parenting strategies of groups of wild boar sows to sheer stupidity: 'the young ones hardly know their mothers, for they are very apt to mistake her, and to suck the first sow that will permit them.'

However, Buffon does credit wild boar with some intelligence when he describes their defence against attack by wolves: 'they form themselves into flocks, and if attacked, the largest and strongest front the enemy, and by pressing against the weak ones keep them in the middle.' He also notes their habit of digging 'nearly in a straight line', unlike domestic pigs, which produce irregular furrows, and their liking for 'new-dug clay', which they will lick and swallow in great quantities (presumably because it contains beneficial minerals).[11]

Charles Darwin considered boar in his book *The Variation of Animals and Plants under Domestication* (1868). As he tried to account for the differences in physique between wild boar and

Georges-Louis Leclerc, Comte de Buffon, 'Le marcassin', from *Histoire naturelle* (1766).

domesticated pigs, he struggled to impose order on the mass of examples he had collected from all round the world, from the 'feral pigs' of Jamaica with their plumed tails to the gaunt 'Irish Greyhound pig' and the wild pigs of Eagle Islet in the Falklands with bristly ridged backs and large tusks. The variety was amazing, and the line between wild and tame hard to draw, especially as some isolated populations of farmed animals had preserved ancestral traits – such as the pigs of the Orkney Islands, with their 'erect and sharp ears'. Darwin wondered why the face of the domestic pig is much broader and shorter than the wild boar's, and examined a previous theory that wild boar, 'in ploughing up the ground with their muzzles, have, whilst young, to exert the powerful muscles fixed to the hinder part of the head'. When

Charles Darwin's illustration of the head of a wild boar and of 'Golden Days', a pig of the Yorkshire Large Breed, from *The Variation of Animals and Plants under Domestication* (1868).

Paul Bransom,
'Wild Boar',
from *An Argosy
of Fables* (1921),
ed. F. T. Cooper.

they no longer need to do this, because they are fed by the farmer,
'the back of the skull becomes modified in shape'. Darwin was
not entirely convinced by this argument, but he did think that
the disappearance of tusks and bristles in domestic pigs was due
to the fact that, living under shelter, they no longer needed such
protection. He noted that once populations of pigs reverted to a
feral state, the tusks and bristles rapidly reappeared. The 'wild'
template of the boar was impossible to erase permanently.[12]

3 The Legendary Boar

Boars appear in myths and legends from many different cultures. The Hindu god Vishnu was incarnated as the boar Varaha, the third of his ten avatars. Vishnu as Varaha saves the Earth when the demon Hiranyaksha immerses it in the primordial ocean; Varaha raises the Earth on his tusks and restores its personification, the goddess Bhudevi, to her proper place in the universe. Some images of Varaha show him as a boar, while in others he has a boar's head on a human body.

In Japan the Shinto Go'o shrine in Kyoto commemorates the three hundred spirit-boars who appeared to escort the loyal court official Wake no Kiyomaro (733–799) as he journeyed to the Usa Hachiman shrine to pray for advice concerning the imperial succession. Although statues of lion-dogs more commonly stand at the entrance to shrines, here they are replaced by a pair of stone boars. Every November the shrine hosts a Boar Festival, which is attended by many who have leg injuries as well as those praying for safe journeys, since the wounds on Wake no Kiyomaro's legs – in some versions of the story his enemies had sliced through his sinews – were miraculously healed by his guardian boars. The boar is also one of the animals in the Japanese – and Chinese – zodiac: those born during its year are said to be determined and impetuous.

In the West, the boar came to be associated with various mystery cults, including that of the god Adonis, who was killed by a

Vahara, avatar of Vishnu, 11th-century north Indian sculpture.

wild boar. Boars were linked with darkness, death and the turning of the year, and might represent vegetation deities such as the Celtic god Moccus, in whose honour boar-flesh was mixed with seed corn and buried in the fields to ensure a good harvest. They were also ridden on by gods, such as the Celtic goddess Arduinna, guardian of the wild Ardennes forest, whose cult later mingled with that of the Roman goddess Diana.

However, it was the boar's role as the foe of humans that came to predominate in Western traditions. In one of the many fables attributed to Aesop, a fox meets a wild boar busily sharpening his tusks against the trunk of a tree. The fox asks him why he is doing that when there is no danger threatening him from either hunter or hound. The boar replies, 'I do it advisedly; for it would never do to have to sharpen my weapons just at the time I ought to be using them.' The fable has had various morals attached to it, from the tendentious ('Preparation for war is the best guarantee of peace') to the hazily philosophical ('Lost time cannot be recalled'), and an insurance firm in the 1930s distributed a blotter with a colour picture of the pair, and a reminder that 'The time to insure is BEFORE disaster overtakes your home or business.' Central to the story is the boar's wariness and foresight, and its (amply justified) expectation that it will inevitably face danger from humans.

In Greek myth, many of the heroes prove their valour by hunting and killing a particularly fearsome wild boar. The fifth-century BC lyric poet Bacchylides praises Theseus' victory over 'the man-killing sow in Cremmyon's woods', while Ovid in his *Metamorphoses* hails 'most mighty Theseus', thanks to whose deed the farmers of Cromyon can now till their fields without fear of attack.[1] The monstrous Cromyonian Sow was kept by an old woman called Phaia, and is an exception to the general rule that the ferocious wild boars of legend are male. The Greek historian

Fujimoto Mokuden, *Kissho inoshishi* (Auspicious Wild Boar), New Year's Day 1983, colours on gold paper.

Plutarch, in his *Life of Theseus*, speculates that the legend might preserve the memory of a ruthless female robber called Phaia: 'a woman of murderous and unbridled spirit, who dwelt in Crommyon, was called Sow because of her life and manners, and was afterwards slain by Theseus.'[2]

Next in line, the (male) Calydonian Boar was supposed to be the Cromyonian Sow's offspring. It was sent by the goddess Diana (Artemis in the Greek tradition), the 'Lady of the Bow', to ravage the land of Calydon after its king, Oeneus, failed to honour her in his harvest sacrifices. The hunt for it is one of the focal episodes of Greek myth, since it drew together a number of the heroes who were celebrated as the founders of ruling houses – the 'best of the Hellenes', as they were described by Bacchylides. Among them were Oeneus's son, Meleager, and the huntress Atalanta, whose presence Artemis hoped would stir up rivalry and discord among the men. Several of the hunters in fact challenged her right to be there, but she was championed by Meleager and proved her mettle when she wounded the boar

35

with an arrow. Meleager then killed it, and offered its skin to
Atalanta, since she had drawn first blood. However, his mother's
brothers (or, in an alternative version, an uncle and one of his
own brothers) took the skin away from her, arguing that, as a
woman, her claim was invalid, and that if Meleager refused it for
himself, it should pass to them, as his nearest male relatives.
Enraged, Meleager killed them; when the news reached his
mother, she threw on to the fire the half-burned brand she had

kept safe ever since the Fates had prophesied that her son's life would last only as long as it remained unconsumed. Meleager fell down dead, and Artemis achieved her revenge.

The second-century traveller and geographer Pausanias viewed the hide of the Calydonian Boar at the temple of Athena Alea at Tegea in Laconia, although he thought it was in a sorry state, 'rotted by age and now altogether without bristles'.[3] It was also tuskless: the tusks had been carried off by the Roman emperor Augustus, and the surviving one (the other had been broken) 'is kept in the gardens of the emperor, in a sanctuary of Dionysus, and is about half a fathom long'.[4] ('Half a fathom' – about 90 centimetres, or 35 inches – is impossibly long for a wild boar: if the relic existed, it may have been ivory from a modern or extinct species of elephant.)

Painted plate showing the hunt for the Calydonian Boar, Italy, 1544.

Pot-pourri vase showing Meleager carrying the head of the Calydonian Boar, *c.* 1755.

One of the twelve labours of the Greek hero Heracles (ancient Rome's Hercules) was to capture the ferocious Erymanthian Boar. Taking the advice of the wise centaur Chiron, Heracles first frightened the boar out of its lair by shouting at it, then drove it into deep snow to hamper its movement. He tied it up and carried it back to King Eurystheus, who was so terrified by its appearance that he tried to hide in a storage jar, or *pithos*. Afterwards, according to one version of the legend, Heracles threw the boar into the

Heracles captures the Erymanthian Boar, seizing it by the hind leg as it tries to escape. Black-figured oenochoe (wine jug) attributed to the Lysippides Painter, 520–500 BC.

sea, and it swam to Italy. Pausanias mentions a tradition that the tusks of the boar are preserved at the temple of Apollo at Cumea, but adds that in his view this is highly improbable.

In Homer's *Odyssey*, the disguised Odysseus, returned to Ithaca, is recognized by his old nurse, Eurycleia, by the scar above his knee. This is where, when he was a boy, a boar he was hunting with his grandfather Autolycus gouged a deep strip of flesh with its tusks. Despite his wound, Odysseus pierced the boar with his

bronze spear, and it collapsed in the dust, 'grunting out his breath as his life winged away'.[5] Autolycus, the son of Hermes, and with many of his father's trickster talents, chanted a spell which stemmed the bleeding, and the injured youth made a full recovery and returned to his homeland, displaying his scar proudly as a mark of passage into adulthood. Many years later the scar serves to confirm his identity beyond doubt, as Eurycleia bathes the legs of the unknown guest.

In Norse myth boars appear as the allies of the gods, and are also served up at the heroic feasts of Valhalla. There the boar Sæhrímnir provides an unending supply of meat for the Einherjar, the heroes who have died in battle. Andhrímnir, the cook of the Æsir (the main tribe of gods), kills Sæhrímnir and boils his flesh in the cauldron Eldhrímnir, but after this has been eaten the boar always returns to life, to provide food for the following day.[6]

The boar Gullinbursti (Golden Bristles) is the steed of the god Freyr, created for him by the metal-working dwarves Eitri and Brokk:

> Eitri placed a pigskin in the forge. He told Brokk to work the bellows and not let up until Eitri had removed from the forge what he had put into it. But as soon as Eitri left the smithy and the other began to pump the air, a fly landed on Brokk's hand and bit him. Brokk continued, nevertheless, to work the bellows as before, and kept on until the smith pulled the work from the forge. It was a boar with bristles of gold . . . To Frey he gave the boar, remarking that night or day it could race across the sky and over the sea better than any other mount. Furthermore, night would never be so murky nor the worlds of darkness so shadowy that the boar would not provide light wherever it went, so bright was the shining of its bristles.[7]

Freyr rides Gullinbursti to the funeral of the god Baldr, killed by the trickery of Loki. His sister, the goddess Freyja, has her own boar, Hildisvíni (Battle-swine). In 'The Song of Hyndla', a poem preserved in Flateyjarbók, a late fourteenth-century Icelandic codex, Freyja takes it upon herself to help her protégé, the simple-minded Ottar, gain his inheritance by proving his claim against that of his rival, Angantyr. Freyja needs to persuade the giantess

Hyndla, the repository of ancestral traditions, to tell her what she knows, and so she rides to visit her, mounted on the back of her hog with golden bristles, who is really Ottar in disguise. Although Freyja greets her as 'sister', Hyndla is initially distrustful, and refuses when the goddess challenges her to a race: 'Now take one of your wolves out of the stable, / let him race beside my boar!'[8] However, she mellows sufficiently to deliver a long recitation of the ancestors of Ottar, which validates his claim. Freyja asks her to give the disguised Ottar a magic potion, which will enable him to remember everything she has said: 'Give some memory-ale to my boar, / so that he can recount all these words.'[9]

In the medieval Welsh story collection the *Mabinogion*, the hero Culhwch (or 'pig-run', since his mother gave birth to him near a pig sty) is set a series of forty challenges by the giant Ysbaddaden Bencawr before he can marry the giant's daughter, Olwen. The chief challenge is to bring back the comb and shears that lie between the ears of the monstrous Twrch Trwyth ('the boar Trwyth'), as they are the only tools the giant can use to dress and trim his beard and make himself presentable for the wedding. Ysbaddaden Bencawr also demands the tusk of another boar, Ysgithrwyn Pen Baedd (White Tusk Chief of Boars), to shave with,

Lorenz Frølich's illustration of the visit of Freya and 'Hildisvini' (a disguised Ottar) to Hyndla, from Karl Gjellerup, *Den ældre Eddas Gudesange* (1895).

Ludwig Pietsch, 'The Norse God, Freyr, Riding Gullinbursti', from Alexander Murray, *Manual of Mythology* (1874).

and it is this animal that is killed first by the band of hunters led by King Arthur, Culhwch's cousin. Arthur then sends one of his warriors, Menw, to Ireland to find Twrch Trwyth; turning himself into a bird, Menw perches above the boar and tries to snatch one of the treasures. However, he only succeeds in grasping a bristle, which rouses Twrch Trwyth, who shakes himself in fury, spraying poison on to Menw and disabling him.

Having located his quarry, Arthur summons a host from all parts of Britain, and from Brittany and Normandy too, and they take ship to Ireland to begin the pursuit of Twrch Trwyth. Just as

Arthur is supported by his retinue, Twrch Trwyth has seven smaller boars to defend him, and his company lays waste to a great part of the country, as well as killing many of the hunters and their dogs. Baffled by the ferocity of his foe, Arthur asks what kind of creature this is, and is told that Twrch Trwyth was once a king, but was changed into a boar by God as a punishment for his sins. His semi-human aspect is shared with the small boars, six of whom have their own names. The first of these, Grugyn Gwrych Eraint (Grugyn Silver Bristle), converses with one of Arthur's warriors, who, like Menw, approaches him in the shape of a bird:

Twrch Trwyth approaches the town of Ammanford. Sculpture by Tony Woodman.

> Grugyn Gwrych Eraint answered; all his bristles were like wings of silver, and one could see the path he took through woods and over fields by the way the bristles glittered.[10]

44

On being told that Arthur will fight for the treasures between Twrch Trwyth's ears, Grugyn is defiant:

> Until his life is taken first, those treasures will not be taken. And tomorrow morning we will set off from here, and we will go to Arthur's land, and there we will wreak the greatest havoc possible.[11]

Twrch Trwyth and his companions cross the Irish Sea to Porth Clais near St David's, closely followed by Arthur and his hunters. The boars do indeed create mayhem on a meandering route through the southern part of Wales, killing cattle, hounds and many of Arthur's best men. However, the boarlets are picked off one by one, and Twrch Trwyth himself is finally trapped, grabbed by his feet, and ducked in the estuary of the river Severn (perhaps with an allusion to the tidal surge of the Severn Bore). His razor and shears (his treasures now number three) are taken from him, but he keeps his comb and escapes to Cornwall, where he causes yet more trouble before finally yielding up his last prize. He is not killed, however, but driven into the sea – after that, the storyteller admits, no one knows where he went.

The magical beast Twrch Trwyth was not invented by the author of the 'Tale of Culhwch and Olwen'. He is alluded to in the ninth-century *De Mirabilibus Britanniae* (Wonders of Britain), in which one of the marvels to be seen is the print on a stone of the foot of Arthur's dog Cafall (or Cabal), made while he hunted the boar 'Troynt', and in fact he is part of a corpus of stories about giant boars shared between Ireland and Wales. He is remembered today in a festival held for the past two years in Ammanford, Wales, featuring medieval sword-fighting, birds-of-prey displays and a hog roast; the town's shopkeepers decorate their windows with a boar theme linked to the produce they sell. And 'Twrch

Trwyth' was also adopted, in the 1990s, as the name of a Hells Angels bikers' chapter based in south Wales.

In Irish legend, the Wild Boar of Ben Bulben, who kills the hero Diarmuid, was originally the son of the steward of Aengus Og, in whose house Diarmuid was fostered. The boy was killed – either purposely or accidentally – by Diarmuid's father, Donn, and the grieving steward struck his corpse with his wand and changed him into a boar. He also prophesied that Diarmuid and the boar would one day kill each other. To try to avert this fate, Aengus Og exacted a binding vow from Diarmuid that he would never hunt wild boar.

Diarmuid later falls in love with Gráinne, the intended bride of Fionn mac Cumhaill, leader of the Fianna (the warrior protectors of Ireland), and runs away with her, with Fionn and his men in pursuit. Eventually, Fionn and Diarmuid are reconciled and live in peace for several years. However, one day Diarmuid accepts Fionn's invitation to join him in a wild boar hunt, and is fatally wounded by the great boar living on the slopes of Ben Bulben, a mountain in County Sligo. As Diarmuid lies dying, Gráinne begs Fionn to bring him water in his cupped hands – because of the power in Fionn's magical thumb, this will restore him to health. But Fionn's old hatred returns, and twice he allows the life-giving water to trickle through his fingers. The third time he relents and brings it to Diarmuid, but he is too late to save him. The boar, which Diarmuid managed to kill, was indeed the enchanted son of Aengus Og's steward, and, in some versions of the legend, Diarmuid's own half-brother, since Donn's wife had taken the steward as her lover while her husband was away fighting.

Other legendary Irish boars include Twrch Trwyth's counterpart Torc triath (king of the boars), and the boar of Formael, which kills fifty warriors and fifty hounds in a single day:

The description of that huge boar were enough to cause mortal terror, for he was blue-black, with rough bristles … grey, horrible, without ears, without a tail, without testicles and his teeth standing out long and horrid outside his big head … and it raised the mane of its back on high so that a plump wild apple would have stuck on each of its rough bristles.[12]

As Anne Ross points out in her study of pagan British culture, the exaggerated spikiness of the beast's mane recalls the high crests on the backs of boars on Celtic coins and in Celtic iconography generally.[13]

Boars of monstrous size and ravaging habits appear in a number of medieval English stories. One legend tells of a huge wild boar that haunted Cliffe Woods, outside the manor of Bradford, preventing people from fetching water from the well there. The lord of the manor offered a grant of land to whoever might be brave enough to kill it and the challenge was taken up by an intrepid huntsman, who hid near the well waiting for the boar to come and drink from it. When the beast appeared he shot it with his arrows and finished it off with his spear. Then he cut off the boar's head so that he could take it back to the lord as proof of his exploit. However, the head was too heavy for him to carry, so he prised open the boar's mouth and cut out its tongue instead. Shortly afterwards, a second huntsman arrived at the well, and came across the carcass and severed head of the boar. This man was stronger than the first and knew a shorter way back to town, so he hoisted the boar's head on his shoulders, carried it back through the wood, and offered it to the lord. The lord promised him his reward, but after examining the head he noticed that the tongue was missing. He asked the huntsman to explain this, but while the man prevaricated the real slayer of the boar appeared, produced the tongue, and told the true story. He was rewarded with a plot of land called Hunt Yard, just outside the town. Today the crest of the City of Bradford shows a boar's head (missing its tongue) on top of a well, and the legend is also commemorated in a plaque at Hunt Yard and a mural above the entrance to Bradford City Hall. Pleasingly, Boar's Well itself is now an Urban Wildlife Reserve. The same tale of a missing tongue is also found in Bishop Auckland, where a knight called Pollard dispatches the monster boar at Brancepeth ('Brawn's Path') and is rewarded by the Bishop of Durham with the land ('Pollard's Land') that still bears his name today.

In other local tales, heroes – and heroines – step in to save their lords from furious wild boars and are rewarded with grants of arms or land. A boar that charged at Henry VIII while he was hunting in Sutton Park, Warwickshire, was felled by an arrow through the heart. When the king appealed for the marksman to come forward, he was astonished when his rescuer proved to be a beautiful young woman. When he heard that her family had been dispossessed of their property, Henry ordered it to be restored to them, and added as a personal gift his badge of the Tudor rose, with its red and white petals, which he said should now be the emblem of Sutton Coldfield, the home town of the young huntress. Whether or not the story is true, the king certainly granted a charter of incorporation to Sutton Coldfield as a royal town in 1528, although this may have had more to do with his friendship with its native son and benefactor, John Vesey, bishop of Exeter, than with the hunting incident.

The boars in these legends mediate between persons of high status, such as kings or nobles, and their subjects, who are rewarded for their bravery in slaying the menacing beast. In a hierarchical society, the tales – like many other folk stories – suggest that one way forward, or up, is a display of outstanding personal valour. The hunter just has to make sure that the right people witness his – or her – exploit.

Another legend, recounted by the antiquarian Thomas Blount, and dated by him to the reign of Henry II (1154–89), unusually features a boar as a victim and as a touchstone of Christian virtue. According to Blount, two local noblemen and a gentleman free-holder met to hunt boar 'in a certain wood or desart called Eskdale-Side' (in north Yorkshire):

The civic crest of the city of Bradford shows a boar 'sans tongue'.

> Then the aforesaid gentlemen did meet with their hounds and boar-staves in the place aforesaid, and there found a great wild boar; and the hounds did run him very hard near the chapel and hermitage of Eskdale-Side, where there was a monk of Whitby, who was a hermit; and the boar being so hard pursued, took in at the chapel door, and there laid him down, and died immediately, and the hermit shut the hounds out of the chapel and kept himself at his meditation and prayers.

When the huntsmen arrived they summoned the hermit, who opened the door to them. Furious at being balked of their prey, they attacked him with their boar-spears, mortally wounding him, and then, realizing the horror of what they had done, fled to Scarborough, where they unsuccessfully tried to claim sanctuary. Things were looking bleak for them – but the hermit, on his deathbed, forgave them their sin, on condition that, in future, their estates would be held by the abbot of Whitby and his successors. In this story the crazed violence commonly associated with the hunted boar has been transferred to its attackers, who have to perform a rigorous and humiliating penance in order to keep their lands (every Ascension Day they were required to collect staves from the wood of Stray Head, carry them on their

Lorenzo Lotto,
*St Brigid Welcomes
the Hunted Boar*,
1524, fresco from
the Suardi Oratory,
Bergamo, Italy.

backs to Whitby and drive them in at the sea's margin so that they withstood three tides).[14]

In a legend of an Irish saint, St Brigid, sympathy also lies with the hunted boar. This one runs through the gates of her convent in Kildare, pursued by hunters. Brigid tells the hunters that it has claimed sanctuary and confidently refutes their argument that animals have no such right. Afterwards the rescued boar becomes quite tame, and lives among Brigid's own herd of pigs.

Today, several of these legendary boars, like the boar of Cliffe Woods, are memorialized on coats of arms, both civic and personal. The crest of the Scottish Mackinnon clan, from the isles of Mull and Skye in the Inner Hebrides, is a boar's head with the leg bone of a deer between its teeth. The story attached to it tells how a member of the clan became separated from his companions while hunting on the shores of Loch Scavaig on the Isle of Skye, and had to take shelter in a cave overnight. As he prepared venison from the deer he had killed, for roasting over an open fire, a wild boar burst into the cave and charged at him. He quickly thrust the shank of the deer into the boar's mouth, ramming it open, and killed it before it could free itself. 'Fortune favours the bold,' as the clan's motto runs.

There is also a 'boar' element in many British place names, alluding either to a particular animal or to a once-numerous population. In the Scottish Highlands, Sgurr Tuirce ('boar peak'), near Loch Shiel, is linked to an Ossianic story about an ancient hunt for a huge tusked boar, while the Lowland clan Swinton is said to derive its name from its men's bravery in clearing the area of wild boar. The Saxon name for York was Eoforwic ('wild boar settlement'), which the Viking invaders, perhaps finding it difficult to pronounce, turned into Jorvik (thought to mean 'wild boar creek'). *Eofor*, 'wild boar', is the first element in many modern-day place names beginning with 'Ever-', such as Great Everdon in Northamptonshire ('wood frequented by wild boars'), Everleigh in Wiltshire, and Eversholt, Bedfordshire ('wood of the wild boar'), or Everton ('farmstead where wild boars are seen'). In this way the vanished boar have left their print on the language.[15]

4 The Symbolic Boar

The Roman historian Tacitus, writing in about AD 98, described a faraway northern sea, 'sluggish and almost motionless'. According to popular belief, this sea girdles the world, for the radiance of the setting sun can still be seen there at dawn. The sun god himself can also be seen rising from the waves: 'popular belief adds further that the sound of his emergence is audible and the forms of his horses visible, with the spikes of his crown.' On the right-hand shore of this sea live a tribe called the Aestii, whose language is quite similar to that of the Britons. They worship the Mother of the Gods, and wear, as an emblem of this cult, the device of a wild boar: 'this boar takes the place of arms or of any human protection, and guarantees to the votary of the goddess a mind at rest even in the midst of foes.'[1]

Their latitude of perpetual daylight gives one clue to the whereabouts of the Aestii; a further clue is their gathering of amber from the shallows of the sea – which must therefore be the Baltic. Tacitus considers that their lack of curiosity about this fascinating and highly valued substance shows them to be true barbarians; however, their adoption of the wild boar as a totemic protector must have struck a chord with him, for the Romans too used the boar as a talisman.

A triangular roof tile, discovered in Wales, depicts a running, crested boar under the legend 'LEG XX'. The Twentieth Legion of the imperial Roman army (Legio xx Valeria victrix) took part in the invasion of Britain in AD 43, and participated in many famous campaigns there, including the battle of Caer Caradoc (AD 50), in which the defeat of the British chieftain Caratacus yielded the southern provinces of Britannia to Rome, and the suppression of the revolt of Queen Boudicca (AD 60/61). This legion built the fort of Deva Victrix, on the site of what is now the city of Chester, and occupied it for at least two centuries. Their martial valour was well symbolized by the boar, which was also the emblem of at least two other legions, Legio i Italica and Legio x Fretensis.

Roman roof tile, showing a running, crested boar, and LEG xx.

However, the iconic wild boar was used just as much by the indigenous tribes the Romans battled to subdue. The Knocknagael Boar Stone, carved between AD 700 and 800, is a fine example of a Pictish symbol stone, and perhaps originally marked a boundary, or the grave of a person of high status. The carving is wonderfully animated, with the crest of hair on the boar's back erect, and its muscular shoulders and haunches emphasized in

Pictish symbol stone from Dores, near Inverness, Scotland.

spirals. Above the boar is the outline of a mirror case, a frequently occurring symbol in Pictish stonecarving.

The Knocknagael Boar Stone postdates the departure of the Twentieth Legion from Britain, but during their wide-ranging campaigns they must have heard the hoarse scream of the carnyx, or war trumpet. The carnyx was used by the Celts between about 200 BC and AD 200, and most probably by other tribes across Iron Age Europe. On one of the inner panels of the Gundestrup Cauldron, a magnificent silver bowl likely to have been made for ritual use and dating from the first century BC, three men blowing carnyces bring up the rear of a procession of warriors. They approach a giant, godlike figure who lowers a warrior into a cauldron – perhaps as a sacrifice or as a life-restoring rite. (On an outer panel, the head of a bearded deity is flanked by two smaller figures, each holding aloft a boar.)

The carnyx had a long straight central section, enabling it to be raised high overhead, and a bell in the shape of an open-mouthed wild beast, most commonly a boar. The jaws might be jointed so that they moved when blown, increasing the cacophony; the Deskford carnyx, the only carnyx head to be found in Britain (in Banffshire, Scotland, where it was buried in peat moss as a votive offering to the gods), may have had a wooden tongue which clattered up and down. The Greek historian Polybius (206–126 BC) described the terrifying impact of the army of the Gauls and their carnyces:

for there were innumerable horn-blowers and trumpeters, and, as the whole army were shouting their war cries at the same time, there was such a tumult of sound that it seems that not only the trumpets and the soldiers but all the country round had got a voice and caught up the cry.[2]

At the reopening of the National Museum of Scotland in Edinburgh in July 2011, a specially composed fanfare was played on a replica of the Deskford carnyx. However, questions have been raised about the original instrument, of which only the head has survived. It is made of brass and bronze, and at the time of its construction (between AD 80 and 200) the production of brass was strictly controlled by the Romans. It has been suggested that it is not a carnyx at all, but a Roman military standard depicting a dragon. On the other hand, the details of the upturned snout and the facial folds of skin strongly suggest a wild boar, while there would be an aptness about the instrument being made from recycled Roman metal. Carnyces are borne by tribal warriors in the film *Centurion* (2010), the Pixar animation *Brave* (2012) and Ridley Scott's *Gladiator* (2000) – in the last a barbarian chieftain is shown, rather improbably, using one as a weapon.

The boar, in fact, has been described as 'the cult animal *par excellence* of the Celts',[3] and numerous other artefacts depicting Celtic boars have survived. Along the length of Hadrian's Wall boar artefacts are mingled with relics of the Twentieth Legion, and it is often difficult to know to which of these two opposing cultures an individual piece may belong. Boars appear, sometimes together with serpents, on altars to the god Veteris; scratched as graffiti on coins, often with upstanding, stylized manes; and carved in stone or worked in bronze. Some of the surviving pieces were once helmet crests, and a magnificent boar originally adorned the Witham shield, an Iron Age ceremonial bronze shield-facing from about the fourth century BC, in the style of Celtic art known as La Tène, discovered in 1826 in the river Witham in Lincolnshire, England. The leather figure of the boar has vanished, together with the wooden shield itself, but its shadow remains as a staining on the bronze – a beautifully stylized creature with long slender legs, arched back and pricked, forward-pointing ears.[4]

In Viking culture, too, the boar occupied a special place. It was the mount of the goddess Freyja and, like her, was linked with war and death. The defensive 'shield-wall' was a common tactic of Northern European fighting forces (it is depicted, for instance, in the Bayeux Tapestry); its aggressive counterpart was the 'boar-snout' (*svinfylking*), a military formation with one or two leading warriors backed by widening lines of men in a triangular arrangement. The *svinfylking* was intended to deliver an overwhelming shock to the enemy: however, if the initial charge failed, the unit immediately became vulnerable to flanking attacks. It was a last-ditch throw, mimicking the explosive fury of the cornered boar.

The significance of the boar in early Norse culture is also attested by the number of helmets with boar crests that have survived. Such helmets are depicted on the Gundestrup Cauldron,

A modern re-enactor portrays an ancient Celt carrying a carnyx.

66. *Bronsplåt med upphöjda figurer. Öl.* ¼.

and the design continued to be popular for several centuries afterwards. The metallic matrix from a helmet discovered on the
Swedish island of Öland, and dated to about AD 600, shows a pair
of warriors bearing large boar figures, with prominent tusks and
curled tails, on their helmets. In Britain, the seventh-century
Benty Grange helmet, excavated in 1848 from an Anglo-Saxon
burial mound near Monyash, Derbyshire, and reconstructed by
experts at the British Museum in 1986, is topped by a small iron
boar about 9 centimetres (3.5 in.) long and 5 centimetres (2 in.)
high. Its hollow body, decorated with silver studs, has a dorsal
cavity, presumably to allow a crest of bristles to be fitted. Oval
silver-gilt plates form the haunches, shoulders and tail, while the
tusks and muzzle are gilded and the small angry-red eyes are

Copper-alloy figure of a boar, cast with punched eye markings; possibly from a helmet, 6th–7th century.

garnets set in beaded gold collars. Intriguingly, the pagan symbol of the boar is allied with a Christian silver cross on the nose-guard. The Pioneer helmet, found at Wollaston, Northamptonshire (at a quarry site operated by Pioneer Aggregates; it is also known as the Wollaston or Northamptonshire helmet), dates from the same period, and accompanied the burial of a young man – it too is decorated with an iron boar crest.

The Old English epic poem *Beowulf*, composed sometime between the eighth and the early eleventh century, tells a story set in late fifth- or early sixth-century Scandinavia. The hero Beowulf and his men come to the aid of the Danish king, Hroth-gar, whose mead-hall has been attacked by the monster Grendel, a descendant of the first murderer, Cain. As they disembark from their ship, the poet describes their helmets:

> boar-figures shone
> above their cheek-guards, adorned with gold,
> shining and fire-hard – the war-minded one
> kept life-watch over the fierce ones.[5]

Here the boar's courage and aggression are invoked to protect the human warriors who share its qualities. Once Beowulf has killed

Grendel, there is feasting in the great hall of Heorot, and Hrothgar's bard honours the hero with the tale of Finnsburh, in which a group of Danish warriors avenged themselves upon the Frisian king Finn for his killing of their leader, Hnæf. After Hnæf's death, there was an uneasy truce between the parties while the chief's funeral pyre was made ready: beside his blood-stained mailshirt, his followers laid 'the all-golden swine, the boar hard as iron' – perhaps the effigy from his helmet, or from the 'boar-crested standard' which is mentioned later in the poem.

The celebrations at Heorot prove to be premature, for in the night, while the warriors sleep on bedding laid out in the hall, Grendel's vengeful mother bursts in. Although the poet declares that she inspires less fear because she is a woman and not a man, she is still utterly terrifying. Amid the panic she causes, 'nobody thought about helmets' – this abandonment of protection is linked with the image of death as the shearing off of a boar crest by a bloody sword. Grendel's mother seizes Hrothgar's most valued counsellor, Aeschere, and escapes to the fen with him, prompting Beowulf's next great exploit.

Sutton Hoo, near Woodbridge in Suffolk, is the site of one of the most magnificent archaeological finds in England – an undisturbed ship-burial of the early seventh century. The body, which has now vanished, consumed by the acidic soil, was certainly that of a man of high status, possibly the East Anglian king Rædwald. An ensemble of superbly crafted objects, found in the upper body area – a gold buckle, two identical shoulder clasps and a purse lid – showcase the skill of a master goldsmith. The shoulder clasps originally held together the two halves of a leather cuirass, a suit of body armour protecting the front and the back of the torso. Each hinges upon a chained pin, and is ornamented with overlapped pairs of wild boars worked in gold and ruby-red garnets.

The grave also contained a helmet, damaged when the burial chamber collapsed, but painstakingly reconstructed. The helmet's face-mask can be 'read' as the human face it protected, with eye sockets, eyebrows, moustache, mouth and nose. Each of the copper alloy eyebrows ends in a gilded boar's head. Yet it can also be viewed as an upward-soaring bird or dragon, with the moustache the tail, the nose the body and the eyebrows the wings. The creature's head extends up the brow to meet the descending head of another animal, wonderfully expressing a totemic interlace of human and animal spirits.[6]

In medieval Europe, the adoption of guardian animals was formalized in the traditions of heraldry. Heraldry had its origins in the first half of the twelfth century, when knights started to bear motifs on their shields so that they could be distinguished from one another in wars or in tournaments. It developed into

Sutton Hoo shoulder clasp, with overlapping figures of wild boars, early 7th century.

Sutton Hoo
helmet; each
eyebrow ends in a
gilded boar's head,
early 7th century.

an intricate corpus of rules and regulations, much of which has survived to the present day. Rolls of Arms, prepared by heralds, listed the bearings of individual noblemen.

Boars were a popular heraldic device, no doubt because of their association with fierceness in battle, and the fact that their tusks and dorsal crest made them easily identifiable. The white boar, which was the device of Richard of York, Duke of Gloucester, later Richard III (*r.* 1483–5), may also suggest wordplay, since the medieval spelling 'bore' is an anagram of Ebor, or York.

Two white boars support his arms in a stained-glass window in York Minster. However, a heraldic device could also be turned against its bearer by his enemies, and in Richard's case this took a particularly elaborate form.

Shakespeare's play *Richard III* is a demolition job on the monarch's reputation, and a political hymn of praise to his (Tudor) successor, Henry VII. To his enemies Richard is a 'wretched, bloody, and usurping boar' (V.2), whose evil deeds destabilize the realm of England in the same way that a boar churns up the ground with its tusks – 'the greatest harm that commeth by Swine is in rooting and turning up of the earth', as Edward Topsell puts it.[7] 'The crook-backed Boar the way hath found / To root our Roses from our ground', says one of the characters in Thomas Heywood's play *The First and Second Parts of King Edward IV* (1600), apparently quoting a current 'slanderous rhyme' about Richard's destructive role in the Wars of the Roses, between the rival houses of York and Lancaster.[8] The true extent of the king's spinal deformity has been debated, but it was a well-established fact for Shakespeare's audience, and in *Richard III* his bitter foe, Queen Margaret, who has already jeered at him as an 'elvish-marked, abortive rooting-hog', mocks his hunched ('bunched-back') body, linking it again with the boar, 'whose back is likewise rounded, lumpy, and punctuated with bristles' (I.3).[9]

There was also a tradition that Richard was born with a full set of teeth, an anomaly that made him even more boar-like, for, as George Gascoigne wrote in *The Noble Art of Venerie*, 'When his Dame doth pigge him, [the boar] hath as many teeth as ever he will have.'[10] Richard's teeth, of course, are employed for no good purpose: 'Teeth hadst thou in thy head when thou wast born / To signify thou camest to bite the world', as King Henry VI accuses him in *Henry VI, Part 3*, just before he himself is murdered by Richard (V.6).[11]

Richard's many enemies draw upon other traditional images as they present him as the death-dealing boar in *Richard III*. 'He dreamt tonight the boar had razed [slashed] his helm' (III.2), a messenger reports to Lord Hastings of his master, Lord Stanley, perhaps with a glance back to the 'life-watch' kept by the boar crest once worn by warriors on their helmets. Hastings is not convinced, and counters with an observation drawn from hunting:

> To fly the boar before the boar pursues us
> Were to incense the boar to follow us
> And make pursuit where he did mean no chase.

If Stanley is intent on confronting 'the boar', he should at least go well prepared: 'What, my lord, where is your boar-spear, man? / Fear you the boar, and go so unprovided?'

Shakespeare's play shows us a scheming, demonic Richard, and is not to be read as straight history. What is certain is that Richard's device was the white boar, and that he gave badges bearing this symbol to his supporters to wear as a sign of their allegiance. This was a common practice: Richard II, for example, distributed numerous copies of his badge of the white hart. In the Wilton Diptych, a small portable altarpiece which shows the king presented by three saints to the Virgin and Child and angels, even the angels have small white harts pinned to their blue robes. At Richard III's coronation in 1483, he gave away many boar badges, according to the royal wardrobe accounts for that year. Most would have been made of cloth, or a cheap metal such as lead or pewter, but some, intended for his most valued supporters, were silver-gilt, and a few of these have survived.

One, the Chiddingly badge, now in the British Museum, was found in Chiddingly in East Sussex in 1999. Although the boar's snout and forelimbs have broken off, its tusks and crest are clearly

Copper-alloy
boar badge
found on
the Thames
foreshore, late
15th century.

visible. There are tracings of a fixing on the back, so it may have been pinned to a hat or to clothing. Another badge, this time made of copper-alloy, was found on the Thames foreshore, near the Tower of London, in 2012. Its boar is chained and collared and wears a crown. A crescent moon at the top of its right foreleg shows that its owner was a second son, but nothing more is known of him, beyond the fact that he too was one of Richard's supporters.

The Bosworth boar badge, found in 2009, is similar to the Chiddingly badge, but has a particular historical resonance, since it was retrieved from the edge of Fen Hole, medieval marshland close to the site of the last, decisive action of the Wars of the Roses, the Battle of Bosworth Field, in which Richard was killed on 2 August 1485. He was the last English king to be killed in battle, and his death marked the end of the Plantagenet dynasty and the accession of the Tudors, with the victor, Henry Tudor, becoming Henry VII.

Historians have long debated the exact site of the battle, and, in particular, the spot where the king was killed. The chroniclers of the time wrote that he was hacked to death when his horse became bogged down in marshland. The contemporary Welsh poet Guto'r Glyn (the Tudors were a Welsh dynasty) hailed the man who 'killed the boar, shaved his head', and certainly the body of the king, discovered buried under a car park in Leicester in 2012, had gaping wounds in its skull, which must have proved fatal.[12]

The Bosworth boar badge was definitely worn by a person of high status, perhaps one of the knights who rode with the king and tried to defend him to the last. As with the Chiddingly badge, there are signs of a fixing on the back. The silver boar may have been worn as a pendant, or have been pinned to the silk covering over armour which would also have displayed the wearer's coat of arms.[13] Its discovery next to a marsh enabled historians to pinpoint the place where Richard died; it has certainly prompted a rethink of the whole topography of the battlefield. Today the battle of Bosworth Field is commemorated in the coat of arms of the borough of Hinckley and Bosworth, on the crest of which a red dragon (the emblem of Henry Tudor) subdues Richard's white boar.

Guto'r Glyn praises the man who 'killed the boar', and, as we have seen, some writers play with the extent to which the bearer of arms can be identified with his heraldic symbol. 'To bere a boore in armes', one of the heraldic manuscripts reads, 'hyt betokeneth . . . a sotell and strong warrior, wiche will rather dye in batell than be fleing awaye to saue [save] his lyfe.'[14] Richard was just such a 'boar' – 'brutish, stubborne, and yet courageous; wrathfull and furious', in Topsell's characterization of the beast: the sources agree that he fought courageously, killing Henry Tudor's standard bearer and battling to within a sword's length of Henry himself.

Sir Thopas, the hero of Geoffrey Chaucer's Canterbury Tale of that name, also bears the device of a boar – a boar's head this time – on his shield. However, he is a knight of a very different sort from his fearless contemporaries. Chaucer's tale is told in the six-line rhyming stanzas in which romances were often set, but it makes gentle fun of romance conventions by presenting its hero not as a doughty warrior but as a much more cautious soul, who beats a hasty retreat as soon as a giant starts hurling stones at him.[15]

Sir Thopas's device could have a different interpretation, for the boar's head was a traditional symbol of hospitality. The practice of serving one at a feast may have originated in the sacrifice of a wild boar to the Norse god Freyr at the winter solstice, but by the Middle Ages it was common all over Europe. *The Marriage at Cana*, by Hieronymus Bosch (*c.* 1450–1516), shows a swan and a boar's head being carried on gold platters, apparently spitting fire from their mouths (perhaps small fireworks were used). Today, 'The Boar's Head' is a popular name for pubs and inns

The Bosworth boar badge, late 15th century.

(dating as far back as Shakespeare's Boar's Head tavern in East-cheap, London, where Falstaff and his friends caroused, under the eye of the landlady, Mistress Quickly), while the Boar's Head Provision Company, founded in New York in 1905, delivers meats, cheeses and condiments all over the United States.

At The Queen's College, Oxford, the Boar's Head Feast has long been celebrated. It began as a Christmas dinner for members of the college, and may reflect Scandinavian influence through the college's early connection with the northern counties of Cumberland and Westmorland, from which many of its students were drawn. A boar's head, decorated with sprays of herbs and small heraldic flags, is borne into the hall, accompanied by the college choir, who sing the Boar's Head Carol:

> The boar's head in hand bring I,
> Bedeck'd with bays and rosemary.
> And I pray you, my masters, be merry
> *Quot estis in convivio* [As many as are in the feast].

> CHORUS:
> *Caput apri defero* [The boar's head I offer]
> *Reddens laudes Domino* [Giving praises to the Lord].

> The boar's head, as I understand,
> Is the rarest dish in all this land,
> Which thus bedeck'd with a gay garland
> Let us *servire cantico* [serve with a song].

> CHORUS

> Our steward hath provided this
> In honour of the King of Bliss;

Which on this day to be served is
In Reginensi atrio [In the hall of Queen's].

College accounts for 1395 show the purchase of a boar's head, which was very probably for this feast (the text of the carol dates from the fifteenth century). In 1961, after a brief abeyance of three years, the feast was revived, and moved to the Saturday before Christmas, when it became a gaudy, or celebratory dinner for former students. During the Second World War, when real boars' heads were hard to come by, a papier mâché model did duty; today a stuffed boar's head is used in the procession.

College tradition connects the Boar's Head Feast with the exploit of a student who, while walking in Shotover woods on the outskirts of the city, was attacked by a ferocious wild boar. With great presence of mind, and with a cry of *'Graecum est!* [It's

A boar's head is carried in procession; illustration from *The Poetical Works of Henry Wadsworth Longfellow* (1899).

68

Boar sculpture on top of a gatepost at Charlecote Park, Warwickshire, England.

Greek!]', the youth thrust the copy of Aristotle he was reading down the beast's throat, and choked it to death. Whether anything like this really happened is impossible to say. The College has on display a large eighteenth-century portrait of 'Copcot, traditionally supposed to have killed the boar on Shotover', but it shows a grey-bearded patriarch in flowing robes instead of a virile young student, and in fact is a close copy of a stained-glass window in Horspath parish church, a few miles away.

A particular aspect of the boar's behaviour, its rooting in farmland and especially in vineyards, gave rise to a further strand of symbolism. In Psalm 80 the Psalmist compares the flight of God's chosen people out of Egypt, and their establishment in their own land, with the planting and growth of a massive vine with boughs like those of cedars shadowing the hills. However, wild animals threaten the vine's survival: 'The boar out of the wood doth waste it, and the wild beast of the field doth devour it' (verse 13). During the bitter religious conflicts of the sixteenth and seventeenth centuries, many writers took up the image of the invading boar to brand their opponents destroyers of the community (the 'vineyard') of faith. They took their cue from Pope Leo x, who had condemned the reformer Martin Luther in such terms in his papal bull of 1520, 'Exsurge Domine' ('Rise up, O Lord'):

> Listen to our prayers, for foxes have arisen seeking to destroy the vineyard you alone have trod. When you were about to ascend to your Father, you committed the care, rule, and administration of the vineyard, an image of the triumphant church, to Peter, as the head and your vicar and his successors. The wild boar from the forest seeks to destroy it and every wild beast feeds upon it.[16]

In their turn, Protestants used the same image to berate Catholics: so, in 1592, Andrew Willet praised Queen Elizabeth I as the

'Syrian Wild Boar', coloured chalk lithograph illustrating Psalm 80, verse 13.

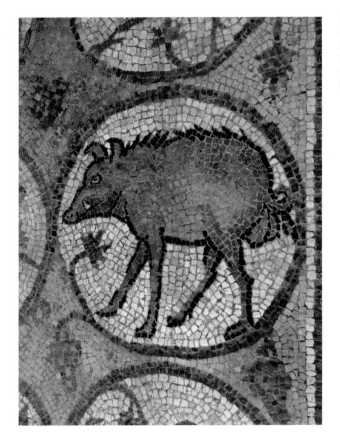

Mosaic of a
wild boar on the
northern aisle floor
of the Byzantine
Church of Petra,
Jordan.

nation's 'hedge', or defence, against papacy: 'The Lord hath made
you a wall and a hedge to his vineyard to keepe out the wilde
boare.'[17]

In fact, wild boar in vineyards are not just a handy metaphor,
more of an age-old problem. In the nineteenth century a certain
Reverend Mr Leeves was travelling to the village of Therapia
(modern Tarabya, near Istanbul) when he saw 'an animal of large

size' rush out of a vineyard, cross the road in front of him, and dash out of sight. The guard who was accompanying him explained:

> 'tis the custom of the wild-boars to frequent the vineyards, and to devour the grapes. And it is astonishing what havoc a wild-boar is capable of effecting during a single night. What with eating, and what with trampling under foot, he will destroy an immense quantity of grapes.[18]

And today, in Tuscany, in the region where the popular wine Chianti Classico is produced, wine growers are engaged in a battle with voracious wild boar who break into the vineyards to eat the sweet grapes, pitting the ground with 'holes that look like Ho Chi Minh trails'.[19] The cost in lost harvest is estimated at more than €10 million, and many growers have had to surround their land with steel-mesh fences, which, as well as involving great expense, alter the appearance and character of the whole area. 'It's extremely ugly, we know it,' says Roberto Da Frassini, technical director of the Tenuta di Nozzole estate. 'It's like building a camp on the vineyards, but what is the alternative?'[20] Other producers have experimented with small, gas-filled cannons, or with machines that emit ultrasound.

In February 2016 the regional government passed a law which allows licensed hunters to shoot wild boar and roe and fallow deer of a certain age and gender outside the regular three-month hunting season, and extends the locations where hunting is permitted to include, under strict conditions, fields, parks, vineyards and even urban areas. The aim is to reduce the wild boar population from an estimated 400,000 today to around 150,000 in three years' time. Yet this law has itself created controversy, with many complaining that the expansion of shooting areas threatens to 'militarize' the peaceful Tuscan countryside. And the hunters have been accused of deliberately baiting areas to attract their prey – vans packed with loaves of bread and containers of corn have allegedly been found parked near vineyards, drawing even more boar out of the woods to an easy feast. 'When I was a kid, if I wanted to see these animals I had to go to the cinema,' says Francesco Ricasoli, winemaker and patriarch of an ancient noble family. 'Now the animals are wildly and freely going around.'[21]

5 The Hunted Boar

Humans have been hunting boar for millennia. They were desirable prey because of the food and other resources they could supply, but the hunt itself also accrued a range of social meanings. Because a full-grown, solitary, male boar was a dangerous foe, overcoming it was a test of courage and proof of a man's status as a battle-primed warrior. Later, when hunting in general became associated with royal or aristocratic privilege, it gave rise to discord, as people saw the woods and countryside in which they lived and worked ravaged and disfigured for the sole benefit of the hunters.

Hunting was a favourite activity of the kings of the Sassanid dynasty in ancient Persia (AD 226 to 650), and in relief carvings which survive, hunting scenes are often juxtaposed to tableaux showing coronations. At Taq-e Bostan, in the Zagros mountains near the city of Kermanshah in present-day Iran, episodes from a royal boar hunt flank a monumental arch enclosing a grotto. Armed with a bow and arrow, the king waits in a boat, while five of his elephants flush out a herd of wild boar, who flee across the marshy lake. Two large boar fall through the picture space, showing that the king has killed them; to the right, the king stands with slackened bow, signalling that the hunt is over. Escaped boar weave through the reeds; below, elephants retrieve the dead animals, using their trunks to lift them on to their backs. Accompanying boats filled with female musicians add to the celebratory air.

In ancient Greece, where, as we have seen, many of the most famous myths about boar hunting arose, youths were encouraged to hunt the boar as part of their training in military affairs and in leadership skills in general. 'I charge the young not to despise hunting or any other schooling', wrote the historian and philosopher Xenophon (*c.* 430–354 BC) in his influential treatise *Cynegeticus* (On Hunting). 'For it makes the body healthy, improves the sight and hearing, and keeps men from growing old; and it affords the best training for war.'[1] The philosopher Plato (*c.* 428–347 BC) agreed, but argued that it must be the right sort of hunting: 'the capture of four-footed animals with the help of dogs and horses and by your own exertions, when you hunt in person and subdue all your own prey by chasing and striking them and hurling weapons at them.'[2] Far less praiseworthy, in his view, were wildfowlers, fishermen and night-time poachers – the true hunt was a very public display of valour.

François Desportes, *Hallali de sanglier* (Death of the Boar), *c.* 1719–25.

Boar hunt, relief
at Taq-e Bostan,
Sassanid period
(AD 226–650).

Xenophon gives instructions for hunting boar in the tenth chapter of *Cynegeticus*. The hunting party first needs to equip itself with a variety of dogs ('Indian, Cretan, Locrian, and Laconian'), along with nets, javelins, boar-spears and foot-traps. When the likely resting place of a boar is found, a Laconian (Spartan) bitch is loosed to pick up the scent. When she finds it, the other dogs and huntsmen follow, the men taking note of further signs, such as prints in soft ground, broken twigs in the undergrowth or bark scarred by the animal's tusks. Once the tracking dog finds the boar, she will give tongue, but the hunters should catch her and tie her up a good way from the lair (so she is not put at risk in the subsequent action). A strong net is then anchored to a 'stout tree' and positioned so that the sun's rays enter it, in order that the interior may be as light as possible when the boar rushes at it.

The most dangerous part of the hunt follows, as the dogs are sent into the boar's lair to rouse him. 'The noise will cause him to get up, and he will toss any hound that attacks him in front. He will run and plunge into the nets; or, if not, you must pursue him.' If all goes to plan, the combined onslaught of the hounds, and of the hunters, who let fly their javelins and hurl rocks, will drive the boar into the net, where his own strength will draw the ropes tight. Then the most experienced and strongest man in the field should make the kill, with his boar-spear: 'let him hold the spear before him, with his legs not much further apart than in wrestling, turning the left side towards the left hand, and then watching the beast's eye and noting the movement of the fellow's head. Let him present the spear, taking care that the boar doesn't knock it out of his hand with a jerk of his head.' If the hunter does lose his weapon in this way, he should throw himself face-down and grip the brushwood beneath him tightly, so that the boar cannot lever him up with its tusks. The boar will then jump on him and trample him, and his only hope is that another hunter will distract it so that he can escape.

The Romans were equally keen boar hunters and, like the Greeks, used nets to capture their prey. A common tactic was to surround an area where the animals were known to be with large nets, and then send in dogs to flush them out of cover. Smaller nets would then be thrown over the boar, and they would be dispatched with a *venabulum*, or hunting spear. The *venabulum* (which was also one of the weapons used in gladiatorial combats) had two 'wings' or barbs below the blade, to stop a furious boar working its way up the shaft to attack the hunter. It remained in use well into medieval times.

In the countryside villas to which wealthy Romans retreated to avoid the heat and hustle of the city, hunting was viewed as a prime leisure activity. Many of the mosaics that decorated these villas feature hunting scenes: for example, at the Villa Romana del Casale in Piazza Armerina, Sicily, a well-preserved floor mosaic shows a hunter lying on the ground wounded, while his companion stabs at an onrushing boar with a characteristic boar-spear. A collared mastiff confronts the enemy, and another dog snaps at its hind legs. Elsewhere a dead boar is shown trussed in a net and suspended from a pole carried between two men, while a dog prances along below.

However, some Roman writers poked fun at the whole macho business of boar hunting. The poet Horace (65–8 BC) mocked hunters who exposed themselves to harsh weather and terrain: 'Amid Lucanian snows you sleep well-booted, that I may have a boar for dinner.'[3]

> If he who dines well, lives well, then – 'tis daybreak, let's be off, whither the palate guides us. Let us fish, let us hunt, like Gargilius in the story. At dawn of day he would bid his slaves with hunting-nets and spears pass through the throng in the crowded Forum, that in the sight of that same throng one mule of all the train might bring home a boar he had purchased.[4]

Wild boar carried by hunters; mosaic from Piazza Armerina, Sicily.

Horace's 'hunter', Gargilius, duly sends his slaves off at the break of day, equipped with all the right hunting paraphernalia. But they are not heading to the mountains to bag their boar, but to the market, where they buy one at a stall and carry it home on the back of a single mule.

A dog confronts a wild boar on a 3rd-century Roman relief.

Writing to his friend, the historian Tacitus, Pliny the Younger (AD 61–*c*. 113) urges him to take his writing materials, as well as his weapons, with him when he goes into the woods, for 'You will find that Minerva walks the hills just as much as Diana.' Hunting is not a ferment of activity, he argues, but an opportunity for solitude and reflective thought:

> I know you will think it a good joke, as indeed you may, when I tell you that your old friend has caught three boars, very fine ones too. Yes, I really did, and without even changing any of my lazy holiday habits. I was sitting by the hunting nets with writing materials by my side instead of hunting spears, thinking something out and making

79

notes, so that even if I came home emptyhanded I should at least have my notebooks filled . . . So next time you hunt yourself, follow my example and take your notebooks along with your lunch-basket and flask.[5]

Nevertheless, the image of the heroic hunter, embodiment of manly virtue, proved hard to dispel. The emperor Hadrian (AD 76–138) was supposed to have killed a huge boar with a single blow, a feat shown in a sculptured medallion now incorporated into the Arch of Constantine in Rome. Here the boar has just emerged from a thicket, and Hadrian, on horseback, has galloped up beside it, ready to dispatch it with a spear thrust from above. Hadrian was an adept propagandist, and included the boar in many examples of official art, such as coinage. The later emperor Marcus Aurelius (AD 121–180) also struck coins showing boar hunting. In more contemplative mood, he noted that 'the foam dripping from the jaws of a wild boar' and 'the wrinkled brows of a lion' were examples of things that, while not beautiful when viewed in isolation, please us because of their association with 'natural processes'.[6]

When the Romans came to Britain, they found that the thickly forested island was a prime habitat for the creatures they loved to hunt. In about AD 242 an altar to the god Silvanus (god of woods and hunting) was set up in Weardale in the North Pennines, by the prefect Aurelius Quintus, from the nearby fort of Longovicium, to commemorate the successful hunting down of a particularly large boar. This hunt must have been viewed as something special, perhaps because of the destruction the beast had caused, or the valour shown in its killing. The inscription proudly notes that many people had previously tried unsuccessfully to capture it. The altar was discovered by some schoolboys in 1869, and a replica now stands in Eastgate, on the bank of the Rookhope Burn.

A man hunting a boar; 4th-century Roman mosaic from Mérida, Extremadura, Spain.

After the Romans left their country, Britons, and later Saxons, continued to hunt the boar. Admiration for its warlike qualities also persisted: King Alfred's biographer, the Welsh monk Asser, recounts how the 23-year-old Alfred led a charge against the Danish invaders at the Battle of Ashdown in 871, while his brother, King Æthelred, was closeted in his tent, praying and hearing Mass. Alfred fell upon the Danes 'with the rush of a wild boar', and Asser's approval of his impetuosity, which led to victory once Æthelred's forces at last joined his, is shown in his comment that Alfred 'relied upon God's counsel and trusted to His aid'.[7]

In the late tenth century, Abbot Aelfric of Eynsham's *Colloquy*, a manual intended to help students speak Latin, presents conversations with various workers – ploughman, shepherd, fisherman,

Wild boar in a forest; manuscript illumination from Brittany, France, c. 1430–40.

baker and so on – who describe their trades. Yesterday, the hunter says, he caught two harts and a boar: the harts were trapped in nets he had laid, but he stood in the path of the boar as his swift hunting dogs drove it towards him, and cut its throat. To the questioner's comment, 'You must have been very brave indeed,' he replies, 'A hunter must be very brave, since all kinds of beasts lurk in the woods.'[8]

With the accession of the Norman kings after 1066, large tracts of England – not all of them wooded – were declared to be 'forest', or royal hunting preserve, and within these areas special laws applied. Certain animals – the red, roe and fallow deer, and the wild boar – were protected for the hunt, and illegal attempts to poach them were punished with great severity. The author of the *Peterborough Chronicle* castigates William I for his greed, especially for his ban on the killing of boars and harts and his decree that anyone who killed one should be blinded.[9] The Assize of the Forest of 1198 increased the penalty: now, the offender was liable to lose his testicles, as well as his sight (although it is unlikely that this, the heaviest sentence, was passed very often). Meanwhile, dogs whose owners lived within the boundaries of the forest were crippled by having three toes or the ball of the forefoot cut off to stop them running after boar or deer. Such maiming was called 'lawing'. Small wonder that the monarch's brutal appropriation of the goods of the forest was among the accusations made by the barons who drew up the Magna Carta, or that the rebels who joined in the Peasants' Revolt of 1381 demanded that all private game reserves, in water, parkland or woods, should be opened up to common use.[10]

Later, the practice of hunting became codified in specially written manuals, such as the early fifteenth-century *The Master of Game*, an English translation and expansion of the *Livre de chasse* of the French nobleman Gaston Phoebus, or *The Noble Art of Venerie* (1575), attributed to George Turberville but actually a translation by the poet George Gascoigne of a French original, *La Venerie* (1561) by Jacques du Fouilloux.[11] According to the manuals, the most prestigious animals to hunt were the 'beasts of venery' – the hare, the hart (that is, the male red deer), the wolf and the boar.

Boars were treated with the utmost respect: 'It is the beest of this world that is strongest armed and rathest [most readily] shuld slee [slay] a man of any other.'[12] Gaston Phoebus claimed

Hunters drive a wild boar into a pit; manuscript illumination from Brittany, France, c. 1430–40.

to have seen a boar 'strike a man and split him from knee to chest, so that he fell dead without a word'.[13] The second-century Greek writer Oppian had compared the bristles on the boar's back to 'the crest of a great-plumed helmet',[14] and the medieval manuals likewise bestow on boars many of the characteristics of a human adversary. The author of *The Master of Game*, for example, frequently alludes to the weapons they bear. The hard, impervious skin on their shoulders is called the 'shield', while the way they sharpen their tusks is likened to a warrior whetting

A hunter and
a dog set off
to track a wild
boar; manuscript
illumination,
Brittany, France,
c. 1430–40.

his sword. In an illustration to the *Livre de chasse* a small 'army' of wild boars, tusks at the ready, confronts an advancing line of dogs and huntsmen.[15] Such behaviour is not naturalistic: wild boar would not 'form up' like that in battle array. The picture says much, however, about the way the animals were imagined by those who pursued them.

In the hunters' combat with the boar, dogs were their invaluable allies. The boars' distinctive scent would first be detected by a 'lymer' (a dog with a particularly acute sense of smell, the

A line of wild boar confronts a line of hunters and their dogs; illuminated copy of Gaston Phoebus, *Livre de chasse* (15th century).

counterpart of the classical 'Spartan' hound) before the whole pack was let loose in pursuit. Medieval hunting dogs were both highly prized and carefully tended. An attendant would sleep with them in their kennel at night to make sure their rest was undisturbed, and the hunting manuals devote space to the various illnesses that might afflict them, and the proper treatment for each. If all else failed, they might even be sent on a pilgrimage to a shrine, and have masses said for them to speed their recovery: details of such a journey appear in the accounts prepared for the French king Charles VI by his master huntsman.[16]

Such treatment is not only recognition of the value of the hunting dog, but of its rather precarious life, particularly in the case of the boarhound. The dogs used in boar hunting were the largest and fiercest breeds, such as 'alaunts', mastiffs or wolfhounds. They wore collars, often elaborately jewelled, and sometimes studded jackets for additional protection. However, these could be ripped through by the boar's slashing tusks, and many dogs fell victim to such fury. French royal hunting accounts from the late fourteenth century include 'eight dozen needles for stitching up the hounds wounded by wild boar'.[17] Gascoigne, in *The Noble Art of Venerie*, advises against using 'a good kenell of houndes' in boar hunting, since losses were inevitable:

Previously attributed to Wenceslas Hollar (1607–1677), *Boar and Mastiff*, etching.

First, he [the boar] is the onely beast which can dispatch a hound at one blow . . . if a Bore do once strike your

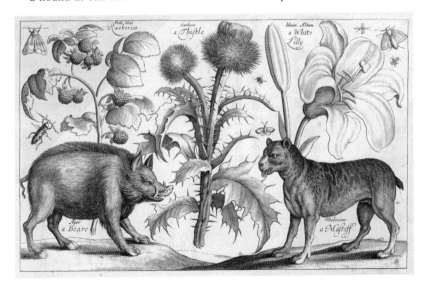

hounde, and lighte betweene the foure quarters of him, you shall hardly see him escape.[18]

The boar's tactics, as Gascoigne describes them, are to station itself in dense undergrowth and pick off the hounds one by one as they are sent in to tackle it:

> And amongst others, I saw once a Bore chased and hunted with fiftie hounds at the least, and when he saw that they were all in full crie and helde in round together, he turned heade upon them, and thrust ammidest the thickest of them in such sorte that he slew sometimes six or seaven in [this] manner in the twinkling of an eye: and of the fiftie houndes there went not twelve sounde and alive to their masters houses.[19]

A further disadvantage of using good hounds to chase the boar is that since the boar's 'hot scent' is so overpowering they are afterwards spoiled for tracking other animals, such as the hare or roe deer.

Still, boars are there to be hunted, and Gascoigne's advice is for mounted huntsmen to surround the cornered animal 'as secretly as they can without much noyse',[20] and then rush at it, striking downwards with their boar-spears. He also suggests hanging bells on the necks of the hounds, since in his experience this makes the boar flee and dissuades it from standing at bay and attacking them.[21]

Once the boar had been killed, it was divided into joints. The cutting up was done in a particular way – to yield 32 pieces, according to the mid-fifteenth-century *Craft of Venery*.[22] The pieces were called 'hastelets' (modern 'haslets'), a word derived from *hasta*, the Latin for 'spear'. A fire would be lit, and the intestines,

An archer shoots wild boar in their muddy wallow, illuminated copy of Gaston Phoebus, *Livre de chasse* (15th century).

together with bread soaked in the boar's blood, would be roasted, and fed to the dogs straight away. This was seen as both a reward for their help, and – since most boar hunting took place in the cold months of the year – a good way of keeping up their strength.

In the 'Boar and Bear Hunt', one of the wonderfully detailed Devonshire hunting tapestries, created in the mid-fifteenth century for John Talbot, Earl of Shrewsbury, and now in the Victoria and Albert Museum, London, the all-too-real dangers of the hunt have been replaced by a romantic panorama.[23] Amid the fashionably dressed lords and ladies who crowd the scene, a boar is shown with dogs gripping both its ears, while the hunters wield characteristic boar-spears with crossbars to keep the animal, and its tusks, at a safe distance. The hunt appears to be taking place

in spring or summer, since the grass is sprinkled with flowers and the trees and bushes are in full leaf. This – like the close presence of the lords and ladies – is an idealization, since boars were hunted in autumn or winter, when their flesh was most flavoursome after they had been feeding on the acorns, nuts and truffles of the woodland harvest.

At some point native wild boar became extinct in Britain. A time during the thirteenth century is often proposed, but it is impossible to be exact, since some of the boar would have interbred with domestic pigs let loose in the forest in autumn to forage

The Devonshire Hunting Tapestries, detail of 'The Boar and Bear Hunt', mid-15th century.

A wild boar falls into a pit dug in an orchard; illuminated copy of Gaston Phoebus, *Livre de chasse* (15th century).

for acorns and beech mast (autumn is also the wild boars' rutting season). The romance *Sir Gawain and the Green Knight*, with its detailed description of a boar hunt, dates from about 1400, but the actual story it tells is set in the distant past, in the time of King Arthur. Nevertheless, its author was thoroughly familiar with the procedures of wild boar hunting, and this suggests later survival. (The Devonshire hunting tapestries were not produced in

England, but in the Low Countries, possibly in Arras, so they cannot be cited as evidence.) In a pair of dialogues between two speakers, a French and English herald, which date from the later fifteenth century, each speaker tries to outdo the other, and the French herald boasts: 'We have all the wild animals which you have, but we have many more, for we have *sangliers*, which are wild black pigs, and wolves and lynxes, and you have none of them.' But the Englishman retorts: 'Item, we have almaner of bestes salvages that you have, and more plente of them to chase; as hartes, hyndes, buckes, does, robuckes and wylde bores.'[24]

Wild boar in fact appear in royal accounts as late as the sixteenth century: for example, the privy purse expenses of Elizabeth of York, the wife of Henry VII, include a payment made on 23 November 1502 to a servant of Sir Gilbert Talbot 'for bringing a wylde bore to the Quene'.[25] When Henry VIII visited Wolf Hall, the residence of the Seymour family, in 1539 and again in 1543, there were wild boar in the nearby Savernake Forest: Edward Seymour's 'Household Book' records payments made to men called Grammatts and Morse for 'helpyng to take the wylde swyne in the forest', for '8 hempen halters to bynd their legs', and for 'drink' after their exertions.[26]

In 1617 King James I was served 'Wilde-boar pye' when he visited Sir Richard Hoghton of Whalley in Lancashire.[27] By this time the native species must have been practically extinct – a situation which could not be tolerated by the Stuart kings, who were devotees of the chase. Therefore, in 1608 and 1611 James imported new stock from France, and released the animals in Windsor Great Park. Later his son, Charles I, brought in boar from a different source – Germany – and let them loose in the New Forest. In their pursuit, James and his fellow hunters rode roughshod over the countryside, frequently trampling crops, damaging fences and scattering flocks or herds of domestic animals. Their activities interfered with the seasonal economy, since James forbade the ploughing of land where he planned to ride (in case horses stumbled in furrows) and ordered pigs to be kept confined (so that their rooting did not create dangerous holes). In defence, the locals could do little more than enact the 'reasonable pretty jest' described in a letter of 1604 from Edmond Lascelles to the Earl of Shrewsbury. At Royston, Hertfordshire, James noticed that one of his favourite hounds, Jowler, was missing. When, the following day, the dog trotted into view, it had a message tied to its collar, which read:

> Good Mr Jowler, we pray you speak to the King, for he hears you every day, and he does not hear us. Ask that His Majesty be pleased to go back to London, or else this countryside will be undone. All our provisions are used up already and we are not able to entertain him any longer.[28]

James was amused – but he carried on hunting.

The released boar must have met a variety of fates, some of those that escaped the king and his huntsmen likely falling victim to local animosity. In the New Forest, just as in medieval times, they mingled with and interbred with cottagers' pigs foraging for pannage. The diarist John Aubrey (1626–1697) noted that they increased greatly in numbers there and 'became terrible to the travellers'. During the unsettled times of the English Civil War, they were all killed, according to Aubrey, but not before they had 'tainted all the breeds of the pigges of the neighbouring partes, which are of their colour; a kind of soot colour'.[29]

Towards the end of the seventeenth century, more boar were introduced, in Alice Holt (Ayles Holt) Forest in Surrey, this time by General Emanuel Scrope Howe: he and his wife Ruperta, an illegitimate daughter of Charles I's nephew, Prince Rupert of the

Ivory inlay on a
16th-century rifle.

Rhine, were the royally appointed joint Rangers of the Forest. 'General Howe turned out some German wild boars and sows in his forests, to the great terror of the neighbourhood,' wrote the naturalist Gilbert White, 'but the country rose upon them and destroyed them.'[30] The accidental, or deliberate, release of wild boar into the English (and Welsh) countryside, and the heightened reactions of local people, is a story that is still repeated today.

Wild boar might have largely vanished from the British Isles, but they were plentiful in other parts of the world, as those who travelled to India in the service of the Empire were to discover. There, boar hunting (or 'pig-sticking', as it was called) became a popular sport among the officer class in Victorian and Edwardian times. 'Tent Clubs' were formed, expressly for the purpose of hunting boar, and rules and regulations written down. The hunters competed to be 'first spear' (the first to strike the boar), proving their claim with drops of blood on the spear's point.

Robert Baden-Powell, founder of the Scout movement, was an enthusiastic pig-sticker during his time in India with the 13th

Hussars, and the author of a book describing the sport.[31] He expressly allied himself with the long line of previous hunters of wild boar, labelling his sketch of a classical sarcophagus showing a boar hunt 'A pig-sticker's tomb'.[32] Pig-sticking, in his view, enhanced companionship among the hunters, made men more observant and alert to possible danger, and even improved relations with the 'local inhabitants', who were paid to act as beaters. In short, it gave 'a mental tonic and a jollier outlook in life in a land where such revitalising is sorely needed at times'.[33] The risk of possible injury to men and horses was part of the hunt's allure: Baden-Powell was quick to pooh-pooh the more pragmatic method employed by 'Kaiser Bill' (that is, the German hunters):

Two Ladies on Horseback Hunting Wild Boar, India, c. 1760, gouache painting on paper.

Robert Baden-Powell, 'Tommy Atkins Pig-sticking'; illustration from Baden-Powell's 'The Sport of Rajahs', *Burlington Magazine* (September 1895).

You dress yourself in a smart uniform, have a lot of stout nets rigged up between the trees, and wait in security behind them while an army of beaters, also in uniform, drive the pig – big and little, male and female – into the nets, and you let them have it with your rifle as fast as you can fire. But that does not always appeal to a sportsman.[34]

The 'pig' himself was at one and the same time innately evil (his 'small, yellowish-red eyes, deep set in his head, give him a particularly wicked appearance, which does not belie his genuine nature') and a 'gallant' foe, particularly in the final stages of the hunt, when 'a strong admiration seizes one for the plucky beast.'[35] 'I don't believe he feels the pain of wounds with any great intensity,' Baden-Powell declared:

and there is no doubt whatever about his savage nature taking a real enjoyment in a tough and fighting finish. He always seems glad to meet you and glad to die, which I cannot recall in the case of any animal of more sensitive temperament. . . . he is well prepared for a rough and tumble life with a sporting end to it, and . . . he would wish for no other.[36]

However, when Baden-Powell came to write his autobiograph-ical *Lessons from the Varsity of Life* a few years later, his tone had changed to a more defensive one:

Chasse du sanglier (Wild Boar Hunt), 1810–55, etching.

You who sit at home will naturally condemn it [hog-hunting]. But again I say, like the drunkard to the parson, try it before you judge.

See how the horse enjoys it, see how the boar himself, mad with rage, rushes wholeheartedly into the scrap, see how you, with your temper thoroughly roused, enjoy the opportunity of wreaking it to the full.

Yes, hog-hunting is a brutal sport – and yet I loved it, as I loved also the fine old fellow I fought against. I cannot pretend that I am not inconsistent. But are many of us entirely consistent? Do what we will and say what we like, although we have a veneer of civilisation, the primitive man's instincts are still not far below the surface. Murder will out. Did we not see it in all its horridness in the War?[37]

Baden-Powell's jumbled rhetoric once more engages the boar itself in enthusiasm for the 'scrap' – but darker words like 'brutal' and 'primitive', as well as the allusion to the carnage of the First World War, betray an underlying unease at his involvement in such an activity.

Today boars are hunted in many countries. The sport is still often one with a good deal of social cachet attached: Pippa Middleton, younger sister of the Duchess of Cambridge, took part in a hunt near Charleroi in Belgium in 2013, as a guest of the family of the fabulously wealthy Albert, Baron Frère.[38] (Belgian boar are noted for their aggression, and dogs used in the hunt wear Kevlar stab-resistant jackets for protection.)

In addition there are companies arranging package holidays so that hunters can shoot all over Europe and in the United States. Countries of eastern and northern Europe – including Croatia, Serbia, Poland and Estonia – are particularly popular since costs are lower there than in France or Italy, for instance. In the USA,

A dog confronts a wild boar in a Russian forest.

although boar are present in most states, the majority are likely to be hybrids, since the animals that were originally kept in fenced enclosures and bred for sport inevitably escaped and inter-bred with feral or domestic pigs. Nevertheless, they are avidly targeted by hunters, and monster specimens – Hogzillas – are especially prized. Modern hunters are equipped not only with impressive weaponry but with customized lures that make use of the boar's acute sense of smell. An Alabama company, In Heat Scents, offers 'Acorn Scent', 'Sow in Heat Urine', 'Black Gold Wild Boar Attractant' (to be rubbed on the bark of trees) and the highly popular 'Grim Reaper Wild Boar Attractant'. Their website features a roll call of testimonials from successful shooters.

The original Hogzilla was shot by Chris Griffin in June 2004 on a hunting preserve near the town of Alapaha, Georgia. Griffin claimed it measured 3.5 metres (12 ft) from nose to tail, and weighed 450 kilograms (1,000 lb). For some time the only available evidence was a photo of the carcass suspended from a rope, with Griffin himself standing beside it. Sceptics questioned the animal's real size (Griffin said he had measured it 'with a ruler'), and pointed out that financial interests were wrapped up in this particular boar: Ken Holyoak, owner of the River Oak Plantation, where Hogzilla was shot, welcomed all the accompanying publicity, with film crews arriving from as far away as Japan. It was also suggested that the boar might have grown so big by feasting on the special fish food dispensed at the fish farm that he ran.

Griffin and Holyoak buried the boar's carcass, since they thought the meat would taste unpleasantly gamy. Several months later, a team of experts assembled by *National Geographic* arrived, to 'do a real CSI-style investigation', in the words of producer Nancy Donnelly.[39] Hogzilla was dug up and measured, and DNA samples were taken. He weighed 362 kilograms (800 lb), and was about 2.3 metres (7.5 ft) in length. Such a size would be exceptional for a wild-living boar, but not for a domestic pig, and DNA analysis proved that Hogzilla was a cross between a wild boar and a Hampshire pig. Far from being a 'mutant', he owed

Hungarian stamp commemorating the World Hunting Exhibition in Budapest, August 1971.

his dimensions to the growth-enhancing fodder on which his ancestors had been fed.

The hunt was on for more stunningly large boar, and in May 2007 another was shot in Alabama. This story's unique selling point was that the shooter was an eleven-year-old boy, Jamison Stone. However, it turned out that this was not a true wild boar, but a domestic Duroc pig (named Fred), and the shooting had taken place in a fenced area on a hunting preserve. Southeastern Trophy Hunters (a company which also offers deer, antelope, mountain goat and Dall sheep hunts, with a black bear, wolf or wolverine thrown in 'for no extra charge') had advertised in April 'a once in a lifetime opportunity to harvest a truly giant boar':

> This monster will weigh at least 1000 pounds - that is a ½ ton of pork! The beast is now roaming the wilds of the Lost Creek Plantation. We are offering this hunt on a no kill = no pay basis. The total cost of this hunt is $1500 and includes everything but the processing of the meat. The boar is jet black and has huge tusks.
>
> Keith O'Neal and Chris Williams will be on hand to help guide and video this hunt. If you have ever wanted to take an animal of this magnitude, now is your chance! This beast will not last long, so if you are interested call us ASAP.[40]

A month later the target boar, which had previously been kept on a farm, was shot by young Jamison, while his father, Mike Stone, and a group of professional hunters looked on. According to Mike Stone, a local TV station had told him that 'if they wanted a news story, only the boy could shoot the pig – no adults'. Jamison shot at the boar repeatedly but incompetently. It eventually died from what vet pathologist Dr Melinda Mercx, who examined photographs of the carcass, described as 'shock and exsanguin-ations primarily from injuries to the abdominal organs'.[41] There was widespread condemnation of the suffering inflicted upon Fred (when any of the men present could have killed him instantly), and the Clay County district attorney asked the sheriff to investigate the hunters for possible charges of animal cruelty. The case, however, was never brought to court. It was reviewed by the Alabama attorney general, who decided there was too little time to prepare it within the one-year statute of limitations. He was also unsure of Fred's legal status, as a farm animal that had suddenly become a hunter's quarry.

The next notable Hogzilla was tracked and eventually killed (mercifully, instantly) in 2014 by Jett Webb, a firefighter from eastern North Carolina. A made-for-television film, *The Hunt for Hogzilla*, dramatizes his quest. Webb becomes totally absorbed in his search for the boar, identifying mud wallows, giant hoof-prints and tufts of hair left waist-high on trees, and experimenting with different combinations of bait. Success comes in the last reel, when he shoots Hogzilla from a night-time perch high in a tree overlooking his feeding ground.

The Hunt for Hogzilla plays up the fearsomeness of Jett's quarry, tracing the animal's 'path of destruction' (when it uproots crops in a field) and interviewing 'Hog Attack Survivors' (a couple who were injured when their car collided with a wild boar). This Hogzilla is a player in a horror film, a 'monster from the swamps' (since the marshy Roanoke valley is flooded with pools of stand-ing water). He is also a 'freak of nature', appearing 'prehistoric' or as though a boar had been crossed with a 'grizzly bear'. Even Jett, who clearly has respect for him, calls him a 'cunning and deadly animal', with a 'nasty attitude'.

No doubt more Hogzillas will be discovered, and more items added to the online gallery of Hogzilla photographs, of hunters

beside their enormous prey. (It is worth mentioning, though, that in these photographs the boar is often made to appear bigger than it really is by the simple trick of placing the trophy animal close to the camera lens and those posing with it slightly further back.) The myth of heroic combat between lone warrior and fearsome boar has proved remarkably durable, but today's technology has gifted humans with a decisive advantage.

6 Boars Portrayed

Boars appear among the very earliest examples of human artistic expression. On the ceiling of the cave of Altamira in Spain a boar is shown alongside steppe bison, horses and a doe, its eight legs possibly suggesting rapid movement. These expressive paintings in ochre and charcoal date from the Upper Palaeolithic era, perhaps from the very emergence of *Homo sapiens* as a distinct species. In the Neolithic mountain sanctuary of Göbekli Tepe (now in southeastern Turkey), bas-relief carvings of wild boars with enormous heads and tusks appear in 'the circle of boars', one of four such complexes, in which lions, bulls, foxes, gazelles and donkeys, snakes and insects, and birds, particularly vultures, are also depicted. Such a variety of wildlife suggests that the area – now barren – must once have been thickly forested.

The hunted boar appears on many ancient Greek, Hellenistic and Roman artefacts, including coins, vases and mosaic floors. These images may be read as evidence of hunting practices, for example, but they are often attractive works of art in their own right, conveying the animal's force and vitality through well-observed detail. Among the surviving frescos (fourteenth to thirteenth century BC) which decorated the walls of the Mycenaean palace at Tiryns in the Greek Peloponnese is a colourful and vividly realized boar hunt. The boar is racing through reeds, its speed accentuated by its laid-back ears and by the ochre and black

The Altamira
boar from a
reproduction in
the Brno museum,
Czech Republic.

patterning running the length of its body. Its tusks, red tongue
and black hooves are all finely drawn. Three hounds, pink, brown
and black spotted, with knotted red leather collars, pursue it; the
trio, like the boar, seemingly in flight against the sky-blue back-
ground. Little else of the scene has survived, but at the furthest
edge a hand can be seen aiming a spear at the boar's forehead.

Tiryns is also where the legendary hero Heracles was supposed
to have caught the Erymanthian Boar and carried it back to King
Eurystheus. This episode was particularly appealing to classical
artists – both Heracles' capture of the boar, and the frightened
Eurystheus' attempt to hide himself in a storage jar when the hero
brings it into the palace. A black-figured amphora of 540 to 530
BC shows Heracles with the boar hoisted on his shoulder, while
Eurystheus, cowering in his *pithos*, raises long supplicating fingers
in terror.

In reliefs and statuary Heracles' smooth musculature was often
juxtaposed with his trademark lion's skin; the Erymanthian Boar's

bristled body also lent itself to textural contrast – as, for example, in a bronze by the French sculptor, and specialist in animal portraiture, Antoine-Louis Barye (1796–1875). In a work by the Prussian Louis Tuaillon (1862–1919), who concentrated on heroic nudes, Heracles grips the boar's ear in one hand and its tail in the other, showing off his immense strength by manhandling the animal like a sheep or a goat.

The boars of Greek legend proved to have long afterlives. For example, the Erymanthian Boar makes a modern-day appearance in Rick Riordan's adventure story *Percy Jackson and the Titan's Curse* (2007), the third book in a series which downloads a host of characters from Greek myth and tracks their adventures in twenty-first-century America. Percy – the son of the god Poseidon – and his friends are under attack from skeleton warriors when it bursts onto the scene: 'a wild boar, ten metres high, with a snotty pink snout and tusks the size of canoes'. Although Percy's friend Grover recognizes it as a gift from the god Pan, there is an episode of furious pursuit, until, in a reprise of Heracles' ploy, Percy tricks the boar into charging on to a trestle bridge spanning a gorge,

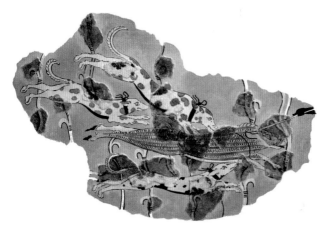

Wall painting showing a wild boar hunt, palace of Tiryns, 14th or 13th century BC.

which breaks so that it tumbles into deep snow. Afterwards the boar does prove to be a 'blessing of the Wild' and provides transport to the next stage of the friends' quest, to the 'junkyard of the gods'.[1]

If the capture of the Erymanthian Boar was the deed of a solitary hero, the killing of the Calydonian boar was more of a group enterprise, involving, as it did, many of the founding fathers of Greek legend. In his *Metamorphoses*, Ovid describes the terrifying beast sent by the avenging goddess Diana:

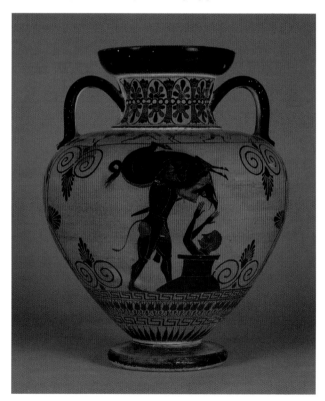

Heracles delivers the Erymanthian Boar to a terrified King Eurystheus. Black-figured amphora, 540–530 BC.

Louis Tuaillon, *Heracles and the Erymanthian Boar*, 1904, Berlin Tierpark.

And the scorned goddess sent over the fields of Aetolia an avenging boar, as great as the bulls which feed on grassy Epirus, and greater than those of Sicily. His eyes glowed with blood and fire; his neck was stiff and bristly; his bristles stood up like lines of stiff spear-shafts; amidst deep hoarse grunts the hot foam flecked his broad shoulders; his tusks were long as the Indian elephant's, lightning flashed from his mouth, the herbage shrivelled beneath his breath. Now he trampled down the young corn in the blade, and now he laid waste the full-grown crops of some farmer who was doomed to mourn, and cut off the ripe grain in the ear . . . The people flee in all directions, nor do they count themselves safe until protected by a city's walls.[2]

In Ovid's vivid account, the boar is tracked to a deep, stream-fed valley, where it is hiding among willows and bulrushes. It charges into the thick of its enemies like lightning struck out from the clashing clouds. The grove is laid low by his onrush, and the trees crash as he knocks against them. The heroes raise a halloo and with unflinching hands hold their spears poised with the broad iron heads well forward. The boar comes rushing on, scatters the dogs one after another as they strive to stop his mad rush, and thrusts off the baying pack with his deadly sidelong stroke.[3]

Although it is struck by a javelin, the boar is not wounded, for Diana, its protectress, steals the weapon's point as it flies through the air. Several of the heroes fall victim to the boar's charge, as it hurtles towards them 'as a huge rock, shot from a catapult sling, flies through the air against walls or turrets filled with soldiery'. It then brazenly sharpens its tusks on the trunk of an oak before retreating into dense woodland. Here the huntress Atalanta succeeds in shooting it behind an ear, but her deed causes further confusion as the men, furious at being outdone by a girl, jostle and impede one another, 'hurling their spears in disorder'. Ancaeus lifts his double-headed axe in both hands and stands on tiptoe, 'poised for a downward blow'. But his immobility, which Ovid links to his boastful pride, is his downfall, as the boar slashes him fatally. It is Meleager who finally dispatches it by plunging his hunting-spear right through its shoulder.

Ovid presents the Calydonian boar as a mighty adversary, allying it both with the forces of nature, like the deadly lightning strike, and human weaponry, such as the catapulted stone. It is proud and intelligent, choosing the forest as its battleground, where its hunters are at an immediate disadvantage. The hunters themselves do not appear in the best light, as they quarrel with each other, or foolishly vaunt their own prowess. Even in death the boar confronts them with their failings, as they gather round, afraid even to touch it: 'They gaze in wonder at the huge beast lying stretched out over so much ground, and still think it hardly safe to touch him. But each dips his spear in the blood.'[4]

In Peter Paul Rubens's *The Calydonian Boar Hunt* (*c.* 1611–12), the scene seethes with action, from the tossing branches of the trees to the blown drapery of Atalanta and the other classically attired hunters and the rippled manes of the two rearing horses. Wounded dogs writhe on the ground, next to the body of the fallen hunter, Ancaeus. But the boar itself is curiously static, although suitably monumental, with erect ears and a luxuriant 'mane'. Rubens intended the picture to refer directly to classical

Sassanid plaster relief of a boar (6th–7th century AD), from Umm az-Za'atir, Iraq.

originals, and copied the poses of several of the figures from the ancient sarcophagi and statues he had seen during his extended stay in Italy from 1600 to 1608. The boar was drawn, not from real life, but from a marble copy of a Hellenistic original found in Rome and then removed to Florence by the Medici in the mid-sixteenth century. From the time of its rediscovery, the statue had been associated with the mythical Calydonian boar, but it presents the animal solidly seated, its hind legs bent beneath it – aroused, perhaps, but not about to explode into action. 'His hair is stubby and clotted, his paws broad, coarse, and heavy, the whole finely expressing the growling ire kindling in an irritated animal', according to the eminent Scottish anatomist John Bell (1763–1820).[5] However, the novelist Tobias Smollett, who viewed the boar in 1764, thought that 'the savagery of his appearance is finely contrasted with the ease and indolence of the attitude. Were

Peter Paul Rubens,
The Calydonian Boar Hunt,
c. 1611–12,
oil on panel.

I to meet with a living boar lying with the same expression, I should be tempted to stroke his bristles.'[6]

The Florentine boar statue was to have an eventful history. It is now in the Uffizi museum, but a bronze replica which forms part of a fountain was sculpted and cast by the Baroque master Pietro Tacca (1577–1640) shortly before 1634, and this copy soon eclipsed its original in fame and local legend. It was first intended for the Boboli Gardens, to join the collection of sculptures there, but was later moved to the Mercato Nuovo, the 'new' market in Florence's historic centre. (The present statue is a modern replacement, cast by the Ferdinando Marinelli Artistic Foundry; Tacca's bronze boar can be viewed in the Museo Bardini.) The statue is called *Il porcellino* (or 'Piglet'), and the loggia, or semi-enclosed hall where trading took place, the Mercato del Porcellino. The story goes that anyone who slides a coin between the boar's gaping jaws so that it is washed by the water through the grating below, and then rubs its snout, will be assured of returning to the city. (Naturally, a lot of coins are deposited by visitors; they are periodically collected and the money distributed to charities.) The boar's snout, in contrast to the rest of its body, has been polished smooth by the hands that have stroked it.

The American folklorist Charles Godfrey Leland visited Florence in 1895 and collected a local story which explains the tiny frog among the water creatures at the boar's foot. A woman was lamenting the fact that she had no children when a herd of wild boar with their piglets ran by. She wished aloud that she could have a baby like the boar, and was granted her wish by a nearby fairy. However, when her son was born, he looked like a boar, although he was both eloquent and intelligent. When he grew up, a young girl recognized his qualities and agreed to marry him; on their wedding night he shed his boar skin and revealed himself as a handsome young man. In the daytime he became a boar again, and he explained to his wife that he would be trapped forever as a boar if she told anyone his secret, while she would be turned into a frog. The ending is predictable, since fairy-tale secrets are never kept, but the boar and the frog still continued to meet at a watering place, and their story is memorialized in the boar fountain.[7]

Hans Christian Andersen was inspired by *Il porcellino* to write his story 'The Bronze Boar' (1842).[8] The boar's 'bright colour', he writes, 'has been changed by age to dark green; but clear, fresh water pours from the snout, which shines as if it had been polished, and so indeed it has, for hundreds of poor people and children seize it in their hands as they place their mouths close to the mouth of the animal, to drink'. A poor boy from an abusive home falls asleep on the boar's back, and, as midnight strikes, it comes to life and takes him for a magical ride across the sleeping city, during which he views the pictures and statues in the rooms of the Uffizi, and the tomb of Galileo in the church of Santa Croce. His experience stays with him, and he eventually becomes a famous artist, his masterwork a painting of a handsome ragged boy asleep, leaning against 'the bronze boar of the Via Porta Rossa'. The message is that great art, and the possibility of creating it, is there for all, rich or poor, just as everyone can drink from the cold refreshing water that trickles from the boar's snout. (In a typical Andersen coda, however, the artist does not live to enjoy his fame, but dies young.)

Il porcellino's most recent appearance has been in the design for the statues of winged boars that top the pillars on either side of the impressive entrance gates to Hogwarts, seen in the film *Harry Potter and the Half-blood Prince* (2009).

By now the Calydonian boar has moved a long way from its original role as fearsome adversary. In the sculpture, and in Rubens's interpretation of it, its tusks are quite small, barely curling over its top lip – a departure from the boar described by

Il porcellino, in the Loggia del Mercato Nuovo, Florence.

Pausanias, and by Ovid, with its magnificent, and death-dealing, tusks. This, as well as the stasis of its pose, no doubt contributed to its metamorphosis into benevolent city patron. It becomes an animal to be stroked and handled, the smooth snout of *Il porcellino* an image of its taming.

Ovid also tells the story of Venus and her lover Adonis, which ends with Adonis's death as he hunts a fierce wild boar. Venus herself confines her hunting to hares and deer, and avoids boars, advising Adonis to do the same, and not provoke 'those beasts which nature has well armed'. The boar, she says, as Ovid repeats his earlier metaphor, has the force 'of a lightning stroke' in its crooked tusks, and is as dangerous as any lion.

However, Adonis ignores her warning. When his dogs start a boar from its lair he strikes at it with his spear, but the beast turns and dislodges the blood-stained weapon with its 'curved snout' and then pursues the fleeing Adonis and fatally wounds him by sinking its tusk into his groin. All that the grief-stricken Venus can do is sprinkle his blood with nectar so that a slight but beautiful flower – the anemone or windflower – springs from it.[9]

Shakespeare took up Ovid's story in his long narrative poem *Venus and Adonis*, the first of his works to be published. Ovid's tale of transformation is itself transformed with a wealth of luscious erotic detail as a yearning Venus tries desperately to arouse the sulky youth Adonis. When he brusquely refuses to meet her the next day, saying that he and his friends plan to 'hunt the boar', she goes pale with horror (although, in her faint, she contrives to 'yoke' her lover, so that he collapses on top of her):

O, be advised, thou know'st not what it is
With javelin's point a churlish swine to gore,
    Whose tushes never sheathed he whetteth still,
    Like to a mortal butcher bent to kill.

On his bow-back he hath a battle set
Of bristly pikes that ever threat his foes;
His eyes like glowworms shine when he doth fret;
His snout digs sepulchres where'er he goes;
    Being moved, he strikes whate'er is in his way,
    And whom he strikes his crooked tushes slay.[10]

Venus's description takes up the theme of the boar as super-adversary, a match for the fiercest of beasts ('Being ireful, on the lion he will venture'). Although singular, it has all the weapons of an army, with the stiff bristles on its back transformed into a row of pikes. As the supreme war-machine, it has also engineered its own defence, its skin almost impossible to penetrate, and its neck – potentially its most vulnerable spot – short and thick. Even the boar's rooting behaviour becomes a metaphor for the deaths it is about to cause: 'His snout digs sepulchres where'er he goes.'

    Venus suggests other, safer animals to chase – the hare, fox or roe – but Adonis cannot be dissuaded. When she ventures out the next day, she hears the baying of hounds, and immediately realizes that they are not running in pursuit, but have cornered a substantial quarry, a 'blunt boar, rough bear, or lion proud'. Their 'timorous yelping' also tells her that this enemy is so ferocious that each dog quails from launching the attack: 'They all strain court'sy who shall cope him first.' Shortly afterwards, she comes upon the boar itself, 'its frothy mouth, bepainted all with red, / Like milk and blood being mingled both together', and then, inevitably, the bleeding body of Adonis, his side split open by the boar's tusk. True to the poem's keynote of erotic fancy, Venus, in her lament, makes Adonis's beauty the cause of his death: this 'foul, grim, and urchin-snouted boar' had only wanted to kiss him, not kill him:

Pottery oenochoe (wine jug), Greek, c. 610–580 BC.

Janet Fisher (1880–1926), *A Fountain in the Shape of a Large, Wild Boar, Sitting Up on its Haunches, in a Square in Florence,* woodcut print.

'Tis true, 'tis true! thus was Adonis slain:
He ran upon the boar with his sharp spear,
Who would not whet his teeth at him again,
But by a kiss thought to persuade him there,
    And, nuzzling in his flank, the loving swine
    Sheathed unaware the tusk in his soft groin.[11]

118

Of all the roles that literary boars are made to play, this appears to be one of the strangest, yet in earlier works, too, boars are enmeshed in erotic plotlines. In Chaucer's long poem *Troilus and Criseyde* (early 1380s), set during the Trojan war, after Criseyde has been taken to the Greek camp and has failed to return within the promised time, her lover, the Trojan prince Troilus, dreams that he comes upon a boar with 'great tusks' lying sleeping in a forest. In dream-fashion, it hovers between animal and human, for it holds Criseyde 'folded' in its arms, while she kisses it. Troilus immediately intuits that she has been unfaithful to him, although his friend Pandarus laughs away his suspicions, and suggests the boar might just as well represent Criseyde's old father, Calchas, feeble and close to death, and embraced by his daughter. The boar's association with strength and virility make us more likely to accept Troilus's interpretation, which is later confirmed by his sister, the prophetess Cassandra. Cassandra recounts the story of the Calydonian boar, a creature 'as great as an ox in a stall'. The Greek warrior Diomede is a descendant of the boar's killer, Meleager, and carries a boar as his symbol. It is he, Cassandra briskly tells her brother, who now has Criseyde's heart: 'This Diomede is in, and you are out.'[12]

Other medieval and Renaissance writers and artists also associate the boar with jealousy and lust, and with violent passions generally. In Gottfried von Strassburg's romance of *Tristan* (*c.* 1210), King Mark's steward, Marjodoc, dreams about a 'fearsome and dreadful' boar that comes running out of the forest:

Up to the King's court he came, foaming at the mouth and whetting his tusks, and charging everything in his path. And now a great crowd of courtiers ran up. Many knights leapt hither and thither round the boar, yet none of them dared face him. Thus he plunged grunting through the

Palace. Arriving at Mark's chamber he broke in through the doors, tossed the King's appointed bed in all directions, and fouled the royal linen with his foam.[13]

Marjodoc is pained and upset by his dream, and even more confused when he finds Tristan missing from their shared room. He goes in search of him, and when he hears him talking to Isolde in her bed he realizes what his dream means – that Tristan is the queen's lover. The dream-image of the rampaging boar both reflects Tristan's strength and prowess, which prevents others from challenging him, and the terrible sacrilege of his deed. The boar's habitual rooting behaviour and the foam it produces as a sexual signal are combined in an unforgettable image of despoilment and betrayal.

In the romance of *Sir Gawain and the Green Knight*, composed around 1400, probably in the northwest Midlands of England, the boar's relation to sexual misconduct is more oblique but present none the less.[14] Bercilak, the lord of the castle where the knight Gawain is staying, organizes three successive hunts – of deer, a boar and a fox – and descriptions of these interlace with the sly attempts of Bercilak's lady to seduce their guest. The boar hunt is the most dangerous of all, since the boar is a huge, ferocious beast who has long lived a solitary life, away from his herd, or 'sounder'. Although the hunters let loose a shower of arrows, these merely rebound from his tough hide, and enrage him so that he charges his foes and inflicts injuries upon both men and dogs. He is pursued all day, and is finally run to ground next to a fast-flowing stream. With rocky ledges at his back, he scrapes the earth, and froth bubbles from the corners of his mouth. Bercilak tackles him alone, in the middle of the stream, armed not with a boar-spear but with a sword, which he plunges into the base of the creature's throat. Once dead, the boar's head is cut off, to be borne in triumph back to the castle, and the rest of the body is dismembered by a skilled huntsman. Its intestines are seared on a charcoal fire, and fed to the dogs as their reward.

The boar hunt is described in compelling detail, but it also plays a role in the wider arc of the story. The previous year, the Christmas feast in King Arthur's castle of Camelot had been interrupted by a great green knight, who strode into the hall and dared the company there (whom he scornfully described as 'beardless children') to deal him one stroke with his axe, on condition that he might return the blow, in due course. Gawain accepts the challenge, and strikes off the green knight's head. But, to the wonder and horror of everyone, the knight picks up his bleeding head, which speaks, to tell Gawain that he must present himself at 'the green chapel' in a year's time, on New Year's Day, to receive, in return, the 'dunt' that he has dealt.

It is while he is searching for 'the green chapel' that Gawain lights upon Bercilak's castle, where, as a knight of Arthur's court, he is eagerly welcomed and lavishly entertained. He makes a playful bargain with Bercilak that the two will exchange whatever they have won over the course of three days – days in which Bercilak busies himself on his hunts, while Gawain, resting in bed, is approached by the lady of the castle, who tries to seduce him. When Bercilak returns from the boar hunt, people admire the size of the animal, and the quantity of meat that may be cut from it – a reminder that perilous ventures such as the hunt are necessary for everyone to enjoy the seasonal festivities. Gawain himself is presented with the great head of the beast, and in return he clasps Bercilak around the neck and fondly kisses him – since he contrived to receive no more than a kiss from Bercilak's wife.

The hunt for the boar reflects the dangers that must be faced beyond the safe confines of the court. It is a creature completely attuned to the wilderness through which the questing knights must travel. Its vitality and aggression, its monstrousness and its final beheading all teasingly echo the green knight himself – Gawain's ultimate opponent. It is also an emblem of the different kind of challenge Gawain faces within the castle walls, where he has to fend off the lady's advances without acting churlishly and causing offence.

Other heroes of medieval romances – Launcelot in the *Morte d'Arthur*, Beves of Hamtoun, Guy of Warwick – also kill boar. Like Bercilak, they face their foe alone, armed with a sword, not a boar-spear – for, as Gaston Phoebus says, that way is more noble (although it is also immensely risky).[15] The combats follow a certain pattern, and in many of them the boar first kills the knight's horse, forcing him to confront it on foot. The romances present their heroes as brave, strong and dynamic, yet also, in medieval scholar Anne Rooney's phrase, 'equipped with the usual courtly graces of the hunter', demonstrated in their proper attention to the treatment of the boar's body after death.[16]

Rosa Bonheur, *Sangliers dans la neige*, c. 1870, oil on panel.

The theme of the huge, solitary boar as the ultimate challenge the hero must face reappears in a number of modern fictions. In Neil Gaiman's *Neverwhere* (1996), which creates a murky alternative London, peopled by those who have 'fallen between the cracks', the protagonist Richard Mayhew confronts the Beast, which is 'some kind of boar . . . the size of an ox, of a bull elephant, of a lifetime'. White spittle drips from its mouth and 'broken spears, and shattered swords, and rusted knives' bristle from its sides and back. The description brilliantly reengineers the 'armoured' boars of medieval tradition, so that this creature's body seems to display the whole history of that warfare.[17]

Russell Mulcahy's 1984 film *Razorback* is set around the small hamlet of Gamulla in the Australian outback, where, in the opening sequence, a gigantic boar makes off with the grandson of veteran hunter Jake, breaking into his house with the force of a tornado and leaving it exploding into flames. The film's barren, sun-scorched landscape, eerie night-time fogs and interspersed dream sequences create a menacing post-apocalyptic mood in which the boar's violence is matched by the brutality of the kangaroo-hunting brothers Benny and Dicko, whose business is turning wild animals into pet food. The boar finally meets its end in their cannery, where it is lured onto a moving conveyor belt and chopped into pieces by a giant fan. Although the film-makers constructed an animatronic boar at great expense, *Razorback*'s scariness is enhanced by the fact that we never get a good look at it – we see either a hulking, fast-moving shadow at the edge of vision, or a close-up of gaping jaws filled with tusks and teeth (a separate, extremely realistic head was also made).

The American author Joe R. Lansdale reprises the theme of heroic encounter in his novel *The Boar* (1998), set in Texas during the Great Depression.[18] The boar of the title is 'Old Satan', an animal that seems to return every few years to create havoc in the small rural community where the Dale family live. It is rumoured to be unkillable, 'an old Caddo Indian medicine man that's getting back at the whites by changing himself into a wild boar', although Papa Dale tells his fifteen-year-old son, Richard: 'I can guarantee you it ain't no demon or devil. A hog is a hog, boy, and that's all there is to it.' The story traces Richard's quest to hunt down and kill the boar. First he learns the skills of boar hunting from an old former slave, Uncle Pharaoh, who claims to be descended from men who once hunted lions on the African plains.

In fact, boar hunting is described in terms very similar not only to the lion hunt, in which the lone hunter 'sassed' the lion until it leapt at him, then dropped to one knee so that the lion's weight bore down on his spear, but to the advice given in the medieval hunting manuals, and in even earlier texts. Uncle Pharaoh notes the boar's tactic of suddenly turning on its enemies:

> He's gonna keep leading them dogs deeper into the bottoms, and then, when them dogs ain't expecting it, he's gonna turn and raise a ruckus. They ain't gonna be able to move him another inch in any direction if he don't want to go. He's gonna pull up tight somewhere, and then he's gonna whup them dogs like a stepchild.[19]

And, if your first shot doesn't strike home,

> the best you can do is toss that gun down and make like an ole possum up the nearest tree. And if they ain't no tree, you just throw yourself down on the ground and pull your legs together and put your hands over your head and try to act like a grub worm by burying up in that earth.

Richard starts his hunt with the legends of the supernatural 'Old Satan' ringing in his ears, and even has a strange dream in which a Native American medicine man transforms himself into a boar. When at last he confronts his enemy, he sees him as 'some kind of evil river-bottom god', with 'a halo of swarming bugs around his head, attracted to him by the stink': 'He had ten-inch tusks that glittered in the sunlight like Papa's shaving razor, and his wiry, black hair looked gunmetal blue. His clove feet were as big as a cow's.'[20]

After Richard has fired the shot that kills Old Satan, a change takes place: 'I looked into his eyes. They were open. They were the same color, but different now. The devil had gone out of them . . .' The boar's death marks a lifting of the enchantment that had possessed Richard, so that he can now see it more clearly – the boar was not a 'dark god', but simply 'a wild hog gone touchy in the head'.[21] Richard has come of age in the same way that the legendary Greek hunter Odysseus came of age when he killed his first

126

boar. And, like Odysseus, he will bear lifelong scars, where the boar's tusks ripped open his hip.

In Hayao Miyazaki's epic anime film of 1994, *Princess Mononoke* (*Mononoke-hime*), boars play a different and more ambivalent role. The action starts with the eruption of a monstrous creature from the forest. It shape-shifts between a host of writhing snakes and a spider, but the furrow it drives through the earth gives a

Siyar Qalam (The Master of the Black Pen), *Two Wild Boars*, late 15th century.

clue to its real identity as a giant boar. The young prince Ashitaka kills the beast when it tries to attack one of the girls from his village, but his arm is poisoned by its black feelers and he is told by a wise woman that he will die from the wound unless he can find healing in the lands of the far west. Meanwhile, the monster, restored to its true form as the boar god Nago, dies, raging against the 'filthy humans' who have not only killed it but destroyed the forest in which it lived. As it morphs into a bloodied skeleton before the eyes of the villagers, an iron ball is discovered inside its body – the cause of its transformation into a maddened demon.

The rest of the story follows Ashitaka's quest for healing, and his involvement in the violent struggle between the spirits of the wild forest, presided over by the Forest Spirit itself and led by the feral girl San, and the subjects of Lady Eboshi, ruler of a fortified citadel where iron is smelted and made into weapons. Although Lady Eboshi's aim is to fatally weaken the forest dwellers so that she can cut down all the trees to fuel her furnaces, and although it was she who fired the bullet that turned Nago (in her words a 'brainless pig') into a demon, she is not simply presented as an evil, exploitative character. Her subjects are devoted to her, and she has given security and employment to those who are outside the bounds of conventional society, such as lepers and girls from the brothels. 'The equation of "nature equals good" does not apply here', Miyazaki has been quoted as saying; 'I have given up making films about good and evil.'[22] Accordingly, the ending of *Princess Mononoke* is nuanced and ambiguous: Lady Eboshi is maimed by San's adoptive mother, the great wolf Moro, but she survives to plan the rebuilding of her town, blown apart by the Forest Spirit's fury. It will be a 'better' one, she says, but what 'better' means is left unexplained.

Miyazaki considers that, at a certain point in history, people lost their sense of the forest as a place marked off by 'a boundary

Mori Sosen, *Wild boar amidst Autumn Flowers and Grasses*, c. 1800, hanging scroll, ink and colour on silk.

beyond which humans should not enter'. 'It was a free and peaceful domain, or a sanctum . . . As we gradually lost the awareness of such holy things, humans somehow lost their respect for nature.'[23] The boars in *Princess Mononoke* are the most dedicated guardians of the forest, which is why Lady Eboshi targeted their leader, Nago. Under his successor, the blind Okkoto-nushi, they mass in their thousands and daub themselves with their own white slaver before rushing into battle against the humans. Although we see them swarming up mountainsides in a seemingly unstoppable tide, they are defeated by the guns, grenades and bombs of Lady Eboshi's forces. A chilling image shows piles of their carcasses. Later, Okkoto-nushi believes he is surrounded by a ghost army of their spirits, but San, who is guiding him, realizes that Eboshi's men have stripped the dead boars of their skins and disguised themselves in them in order to approach him.

The boars' courage is admirable, but doomed. Their 'war paint', or slaver, perhaps allies them with a more 'primitive' human era, before the guns and explosives that destroy them were invented, while Okkoto-nushi's blindness, often emphasized in close-ups of his unseeing eyes, also stands for a more metaphorical lack of foresight.

Most of the boars mentioned so far have been warlike, male and frequently hyper-aggressive. (The female of the species does not seem to have attracted writers' and artists' attention, although wild boar sows can be equally ferocious when their offspring are

Walter Crane,
illustration for
*Beauty and the
Beast* (1896).

Hans Hoffmann,
A Wild Boar Piglet,
1578, watercolour
and gouache on
vellum.

being threatened.) The boar of the imagination is the epitome of wild strength and virility, typically pitted against a heroic human challenger. To redress the balance a little, we can consider the Beast in Charles Perrault's fairy tale *Beauty and the Beast* (*La Belle et la Bête*). Perrault does not actually describe the Beast at all, beyond saying it is so 'horrible' that Beauty's father nearly faints when he sees it. However, it is frequently depicted as a boar, as in the Victorian artist Walter Crane's illustrations of the story, which show a witty blend of the bestial and the cultured as the Beast, with large pricked ears, curling tusks, lace-trimmed costume and feet neatly encased in trottered boots, confronts his intruder in a very human pose of outrage, with arm outflung. In the Disney animated film *Beauty and the Beast* (1991), the Beast is not especially boar-like, but he does have the tusks, as if these are markers of his beastliness. Of course this Beast proves to be gentle and lovable, even while he is still in his ugly disguise.

Finally, after so many gigantic creatures, it is good to look at a miniature example. Hans Hoffmann's portrait of *A Wild Boar Piglet* (1578) presents a self-possessed little creature, with a knowing twinkle in its eye. Hoffmann admired the great Albrecht Dürer, and followed him in composing meticulously detailed studies of animals, but whereas Dürer strove for complete objectivity, Hoffmann frequently animated his subjects by making their eyes more expressive, so they peer alertly out of the frame, meeting the viewer's gaze unabashed.[24] Shakespeare scholar Laurie Shannon speculates that this piglet may have been 'an adopted orphan of the hunt'; in any case, 'The sparkle recorded in the eyes of this young boar . . . records the painter's apt sense that the creature is about to make his move.'[25]

7   Useful Boars

The Roman writer Varro (116–27 BC) begins the third book of his *De re rustica* with the author and his friends enjoying the shade of the Villa Publica while they wait to hear the results of civic elections. The talk centres on villas as productive homesteads, and the friends enumerate, and share tips about, the different types of animals which can profitably be reared on them. There are three divisions: the aviary, the hare-warren and the fishpond. The 'hare-warren' includes 'all enclosures which are attached to the villa and keep animals enclosed for feeding'. The inhabitants of the hare-warren are further subdivided, between wild boar, roe deer and hares, on the one hand, and bees, snails and dormice on the other.

As one of the group, Appius, explains: 'boars can be kept in the warren with no great trouble; and . . . both those that have been caught and the tame ones which are born there commonly grow fat in them.'[1] He describes how, at Varro's own villa, he saw wild boars and roe deer (evidently kept in the same pen) gather together under a platform when a horn was blown at a regular time and food thrown to them (beechmast for the boars, legumes for the deer). At another villa, belonging to a man called Quintus Hortensius, dinnertime was more of a theatrical event. Here the 'warren' was large and thickly forested, so it was more of a game reserve. As the diners settled at the table, placed in an elevated

Wild boar from a mosaic of Orpheus charming the animals, Roman, 2nd century.

spot, a man dressed as the legendary singer Orpheus, whose lyre pacified wild beasts, appeared, and first sang, to the accompaniment of a harp, and then blew a horn. At once a crowd of 'stags, boars, and other animals' poured into view – a display no less exciting, Appius thought, than the wild beast shows in Rome's Circus Maximus.

These animals provided entertainment, but they were primarily being bred for the table. According to Pliny the Elder (AD 23–79), the first person to create parks for boar (as well as deer and other wild animals) was Fulvius Lippinus, who lived around the middle of the first century BC – although Lippinus is more celebrated today as a gastronomic pioneer in the farming and fattening of edible water snails. Farmed boar provided a steady source of the meat that figures so prominently in Roman cuisine. The Latin cookbook *De re coquinaria* (On Cookery), written in the late fourth or early fifth century AD and attributed to 'Apicius' (possibly with a glance at the famous first-century Roman gourmet of that name), gives several recipes for wild boar.[2] 'Boar is cooked like this', Apicius writes:

> clean it with a sponge and sprinkle it with salt and ground cumin seeds. The following day, roast it in an oven. When it has cooked through, pour on a sauce of the meat juices, honey, *liquamen* [fermented fish sauce], *caroenum* [grape juice reduced to a syrup] and *passum* [raisin wine] and season with ground pepper.

In another recipe Apicius tells the cook to boil the boar portions in sea water with a sprig of laurel until soft, and then to remove the skin and serve the meat with salt, mustard and vinegar. He also describes several hot and cold sauces, and a more complicated recipe for stuffed shoulder of boar which was so successful that the great French chef Auguste Escoffier presented it many centuries later, under the name 'zampino', as a prime example of *la charcuterie italienne*. Escoffier follows Apicius' lead in wrapping the shoulder in cloth before cooking it, to keep the stuffing in place and prevent the meat from drying out.

A more fanciful wild boar dish features in Trimalchio's Feast, the section of the *Satyricon* by the first-century AD author Petronius describing the banquet hosted by the man whose name has become a byword for over-the-top vulgarity. Halfway through the feast, the guests are surprised when servants run in and spread coverlets embroidered with hunting scenes across their couches. Then cacophony erupts as a pack of Spartan hunting dogs are let in and career around the room.

Behind them came a great dish and on it lay a wild boar of the greatest possible size, and, what is more, wearing a freedman's cap on its head. From its tusks dangled two baskets woven from palm leaves, one full of fresh Syrian dates, the other of dried Theban dates. Little piglets made of cake were all round as though at its dugs, suggesting it was a brood sow now being served. These were actually gifts to take home.[3]

A servant dressed as a huntsman makes a lunge at the boar's flank, and releases a flock of live thrushes, which flutter about until they are caught by fowlers on limed reeds. 'And have a look at the delicious acorns our pig in the wood has been eating', Trimalchio announces, as each guest is presented with some of the dates from the baskets. The narrator wonders aloud why the boar (which, in an extra dizzying twist, has both tusks *and* piglets) is wearing a freedman's cap (the *pilleus*, a felt cap worn by newly freed slaves). His neighbour explains: 'The boar here was pressed into service for the last course yesterday, but the guests let it go. So today it returns to the feast as a freedman.' (Such greed was not simply fictional: Pliny the Elder complained that, whereas in his day only the middle part, the loin, used to be served at table, now 'it is the fashion for two or three boars to be devoured at one time not even as a whole dinner but as the first course'.[4])

In Japan, thin slices of wild boar meat are arranged on a plate like the petals of a flower, and named 'peony' (*botan*), so that in theory they can be eaten even by pious Buddhists, who are supposed to abstain from meat. Similarly, venison may be called 'maple leaf' (*momiji*) and horsemeat 'cherry blossom' (*sakura*).

Such finicky presentation would surely be scorned by Obelix, of the *Asterix* comics by René Goscinny and Albert Uderzo (although he would no doubt have applauded Pliny's Roman

gourmands). Roasted wild boars – trussed up so they look like monster chickens – are always served at the feasts that his Gaulish tribe regularly indulge in after thumping their Roman adversaries. Obelix himself is an avid hunter of 'Singularis porcus, genus of pachydermous ungulate mammals of which this species inhabits Gaul and is simply delicious',[5] and is often pictured with a boar tucked under each arm. He is appalled when, on his visit to Britain, in a pub called 'The Jolly Boar', he finds one served 'boiled, with mint sauce . . . Poor thing!'[6] The boars themselves are quite small (or at least, small compared to Obelix) and appear fairly resigned to their fate. In *Asterix at the Olympic Games* some of them accompany the Gauls to Athens, where they are assumed to be pets by a hotel owner, express distaste at the room they are provided with (they are 'very fussy animals') and tour the city, admiring sites such as the Parthenon.[7]

So thoroughly are the boars associated with the *Asterix* comics, which in turn can be seen to stand for Gallic nonconformity against the insidious tide of globalization, that there was an outcry when, in 2010, McDonald's produced an advert showing Asterix and Obelix and their friends revelling over Big Macs and fries. One blogger complained that his childhood hero had been 'sacrificed like a wild boar', while the French newspaper *Le Figaro* asked, 'After resisting the Romans, have the Americans finally scalped the invincible little Gaul?' The publishers Albert René, who own the image rights to the comics, were forced to defend themselves, pointing out that Asterix 'remains a rebel' and is no defender of *malbouffe* (junk food). They added that they had previously turned down a request for Obelix to appear in a Diet Coke advert, as the product 'did not correspond to the values of the character' (although a better response might have been to stop digging the hole they were already in).[8]

In Britain, as in other European countries, landowners tried their hand at farming boar to ensure a more reliable supply of the

Félix Bracquemond, illustration for a decorative 'Grand Feu' dinner service: a wild boar shelters from the rain under a plant, French, 19th century.

meat. The enclosures where the boar were kept to be fattened were known as boar-franks; one eighteenth-century author noted a proliferation of such '*Menageries* for Wild-boars' in his native county of Suffolk.[9] And in the middle of the nineteenth century, a Mr Drax of Charborough Park, Dorset, imported two pairs of boar, one from Russia and one from France. He first allowed them to run wild in the woods on his estate, where they quickly increased in numbers, but later attempted to fence them in, feeding them on turnips and corn. He found them 'savage and troublesome . . . to keep within bounds' and therefore killed them.[10]

Now wild boar are farmed in many parts of the world. Farming not only ensures a reliable supply but avoids risks to health, in particular those associated with radiation. After the Chernobyl nuclear accident of 1986, a massive quantity of radioactive particles entered the atmosphere, and were spread by wind and rain over much of western Europe. The radiation is stored by fungi, such as mushrooms and truffles, which are a favourite food of the rooting boar, and the result is that many animals now emit such high levels of radiation that their meat is not fit for human consumption. In Saxony, for example, more than one-third of boar carcasses exceed the safe limit, and since 2012 hunters have been required to have all their kills tested for radioactivity.[11]

In the UK the first wild boar farm opened in Cambridgeshire in 1981, stocked with surplus animals from London Zoo. These were descendants of stock originally imported from France, but later breeders brought in boar from other countries, including Germany, Denmark and Sweden, so that the farmed population is now a genetically diverse one. Peter Gott, of Sillfield Farm Foods in Cumbria, describes how he became a boar farmer:

Wild Boar production started in 1993, when my brother gave me four wild boar gilts as a joke. And it's just gone from there. The farm has about eighteen acres of coniferous woodland – an ideal habitat for wild boar. We now have about one hundred and fifty wild boar stock originating mainly from German and Belgian lines, as well as some wild boar breeding stock with Russian blood in them – but they can be elusive in the woodland undergrowth.[12]

Wild boar meat is denser and less fatty than pork, and is prized as a healthier option. It also appeals to people who are unhappy with the way a large number of pigs are currently reared, in high-density units with foodstuffs that contain additives to promote growth. Peter Gott feeds his boar conventionally, but without added agents; other farmers allow theirs into fenced woodland to forage for themselves. Paul Richards of Woodentop Organic Farm in Somerset keeps his boar out-of-doors in the summer months; they spend the winter in straw-bedded pens, entertained by music from BBC Radio 2.

Wild boar in the UK are subject to the Dangerous Wild Animals Act of 1976. This means that farmers, or anybody else keeping boar must apply for a licence from their local authority and have their premises checked to ensure the animals are safely confined. However, penning wild boar is not easy, since they can lever up fenceposts with their powerful snouts, and run very fast once they are free. The history of wild boar farming in Britain is studded with tales of mishaps, either deliberately caused, as when boar were released by thieves from a farm in Maesteg in South Wales in 2014, or accidental – the great storm which felled countless trees in 1987 also blew down fencing on a farm in Kent, allowing a number of animals to make their escape. The result is that there are now several populations of boar living wild in various regions of the UK. The implications of their presence are discussed later.

Wicker boar, National Botanic Garden of Wales.

Eating them is not the only use that humans have made of wild boar. The Romans enjoyed watching fights between wild beasts in the amphitheatres they built in so many of their towns and cities, and boar, along with lions, tigers, hyenas and bears, were among the animals chosen for combat. A third- to fourth-century AD mosaic from Althiburos (modern Abbah Quṣūr, Tunisia), shows a boar and a bear fighting – unusually, both are named, the boar called Gloriosus and the bear Simplicius.

Today wild boar can be viewed in farm parks and zoos. At Inoshishi Mura (Wild Boar Park) in Shizuoka Prefecture, Japan, they could be seen performing tricks such as kicking a football or jumping through a hoop (the park has now closed). In Britain, Bowland Wild Boar Park, near Clitheroe in Lancashire, houses wallabies, red deer, llamas, meerkats and raccoons as well as wild boar. The boar, however, are at the heart of the enterprise, which began when the father of Chris Bailey, the current owner, started to keep them as a sideline to his business as a pig farmer. Now there are sixty to seventy, and as well as providing entertainment and instruction to visitors they also supply the meat which is sold from the site or offered in the café (for example, as wild boar burgers). When I visited in 2015 I watched a group rootling in the mud under trees – grey-brown, earth-coloured, the male darker than the females who shared its field. There was a lapping sound as they turned up the wet ground. In another enclosure bronze docks and thistles had grown tall, hiding families of adults and their young. Visitors apparently complain that they can't see the animals, despite the provision of a viewing platform, but I followed the guide of a school party, who scattered food and attracted a small group to a patch of bare ground.

There have been a few attempts to keep wild boar as pets, like the German piglet Schnitzel, who is mentioned in the next

The bear Simplicius
is attacked by the
wild boar Gloriosus,
mosaic from
Althiburos,
3rd–4th century.

142

chapter. In Britain today, the classification of boar as dangerous wild animals acts as a strong disincentive (even pet pigs, including 'micro-pigs', need to be registered, and their owner must carry a licence if they are walked outside the home). However, in the nineteenth century regulation was less strict, and a Mr Salvin wrote an article about a pet wild boar sow, originally from Syria, who followed him about like a dog and responded to his whistle. She enjoyed swimming, and runs in the park, and produced several litters of piglets in nests she made in the woods (the only time she absented herself from her home). Salvin noted that she was a tremendous leaper, 'over water or timber. On one occasion she cleared some palings three feet ten inches in height.'[13]

Nor does this mark the limit of the wild boar's usefulness to humans. Boars' bristles have been used for hundreds of years, in hairbrushes and even in toothbrushes. Although many of these bristles will have been harvested from the carcasses of boar, at least one present-day producer of grooming products, Anthony Morrocco, of The Morrocco Method, sources his from living animals, which are 'sheared like a sheep'.[14] Robert Baden-Powell suggested various ingenious uses for the tusks of his trophy boars:

Seiyodo Bunshojo, boar tusk carved with a spider, ferns and a poem, Japan, Edo period (late 18th to mid-19th century).

Small tushes make good labels for decanters, having a silver plate attached to them and being hung round the neck of

the bottle by a small silver chain. A pair of upper tushes make a good stick or umbrella handle, or one single upper or lower tusk makes a good crutch handle for a stick.[15]

Baden-Powell's fox terrier, Beetle, sported a collar made of 'a pair of large under tushes connected by a silver hinge and hasp'. And in the seventeenth century the indefatigably curious antiquary and diarist John Aubrey noted down a piece of thieves' lore: to stop watchdogs barking, they should be fed boar's fat and cumin seed, mixed together in a horn.[16]

8 Boars and Humans

All over the world, in the modern era, wildernesses have been invaded, forests felled, and the populations of wild boar they sheltered either displaced, exterminated or forced into much closer contact with humans. Sometimes, historical events have altered the terms of this interaction. For example, there was a surge in the boar population in northern France during the First World War, as the animals fled from the battles in the Ardennes forests, and a similar increase during the Second World War, when hunting and the possession of firearms were banned in the occupied country.[1] After the Fukushima nuclear disaster of 2011 in Japan, an exclusion zone of 20 kilometres (12.5 mi.) was established around the site, and the bushes that had formerly been cleared grew back, providing cover for the boar and allowing them to extend their range. At the same time, local hunters avoided shooting them, as their meat was thought to be irradiated.

Problems often arise when boars and humans meet. This chapter will look at wild boar in Japan and Germany, and then, at greater length, in Great Britain, to explore ways in which this interaction has been viewed and handled.

Two subspecies of wild boar inhabit Japan: *Sus scrofa leucomystax* and *Sus scrofa riukiuanus*. The latter is only found on the Ryukyu Islands, and is smaller than the mainland boar, as island subspecies of mammals often are. Japanese wild boar have long been notorious for the damage they cause to crops: a heavy blow in a mountainous country where the area of cultivable land is very limited. The poet Matsuo Bashō (1644–1694), living in isolation in an abandoned hut on the southern shore of Lake Biwa, east of Kyoto, mentioned visits from villagers who told him about 'the wild boar that's been eating the rice plants'.[2] And in 1749, in Hachinohe, thousands of people died of starvation during the so-called 'wild boar famine' (*inoshishi kikin*). The famine came about because farmers cleared previously forested land to grow soya beans, which could be sold for profit in the newly expanding cities. In doing so, they created an environment that was ideal for wild boar, with ample brush and bracken and many tuberous plants. These species spread across the fields the farmers had to leave fallow in order to maintain the fertility of the soil (Hachinohe, in the northeast of Honshu, is not a suitable area for rice-farming, and crops of millet and barnyard grass had previously been grown). The famine years also coincided with the prolonged period of cold weather known as the Little Ice Age, when global crop yields were seriously reduced. Massive hunting

Wild boar forage near the Kennedy Space Center press site, Florida, May 2002.

campaigns, led by samurai, were launched against the wild boar, which, equally hungry, were now competing with the starving villagers for the dug-up roots of bracken, arrowroot and wild yams. As late as 1761 the boar are said to have 'invaded the castle town' of Hachinohe, chasing peasants and townspeople though the streets.[3] Today, a traditional saying addressed to young women goes: 'When you get married choose a place where there are no wild boar,' and the boar itself is called 'the king of pests' (*gaijū no ōja*).[4]

To protect their fields, many villagers built 'boar walls' (*shishi-gaki*), and the remains of these can be seen in the Japanese countryside. They were often of impressive length and height – the nineteenth-century Neo wall, in Gifu Prefecture, for example, stretched for 80 kilometres (50 mi.) and was 2 metres (6.5 ft) high. In addition, particular areas would be guarded by men who sat up all night, ready to scare the marauders away, and amulets or charms, often obtained from 'wolf shrines', would be buried at the periphery of fields.

A sign in Japan warns walkers not to try to feed wild boar.

Yet nothing seemed – or seems – to stop the boar. The water-filled rice paddies prove particularly attractive to them, as a Japanese farmer explains:

Earthenware *haniwa* figure of a wild boar, Japanese, 3rd–7th century.

when the rice plant grows taller and gets rough and bushy . . . the wild boars come. They come in July, just when the rice grain is still hard, and chew it to get the juice and then spit out all the rubbish [in the field] . . . They knock over the rice-stalks and roll over in the field to cover themselves with mud.[5]

The boars themselves are credited with almost superhuman cunning, and are said to have a 'thousand-league snout' (*senri-bana*), which can sniff out crops from far away. One farmer reported that they had eaten their way through a field of sweet potatoes but had left the stalks upright so he did not suspect anything was wrong until the leaves started to wither.[6] It is not surprising that farmers consider themselves to be at war with the boar, and use military language to describe their conflicts with them: so the field guards are 'soldiers', armed with a panoply of weapons in their battle against the 'wild boar army' (*inoshishi gundan*).[7]

The boars are implicated in rural depopulation, since perpetual damage to their crops is one of the reasons farmers leave their land and move to towns or cities. Once a farm is abandoned, it becomes overgrown with wild vegetation, which provides cover

Porcelain plate showing a samurai fighting with a boar, Japanese, 19th century.

for the boar and more opportunities for them to encroach on neighbouring fields. They also face less of a threat if there are fewer people about. Boar have long been a prime target for hunters – they not only provide a thrilling challenge but the flavoursome meat is highly valued (especially that of the 'hill boars' (*okajishi*), who feed on chestnuts and berries in the forest)

Tsukioka Yoshitoshi, *Inuta Kobungo Killing a Boar*, Japan, 1866, woodblock print.

and the gall bladder is thought to be an all-purpose tonic. However, like the rest of the population, Japan's hunters are both ageing and declining in numbers. Since 1970 their numbers have fallen by more than half, the *Japan Times* reported in 2013. And, of the 200,000 or so remaining, 65 per cent are men over the age of sixty. Some women are joining their ranks, such as 'Kari Gyaru', who blogs from Tokyo and encourages more women to join her in the sport, while Kentaro Okamoto's manga series *Sanzoku Daiari* (Bandit Diaries), which recounts the author's (fictional) hunting experiences, has enjoyed great success.

Certainly more hunters will be needed if the government is to achieve its stated target of reducing wild boar numbers by half overall.[8]

Japanese boar do enter towns and cities, and have been known to injure people and cause damage there – for example, in April 2013 eight people were hurt by a large boar in Taishi, Hyogo Prefecture, and in the same month an express train in the city of Wakayama made an emergency stop after it hit one that had strayed onto the tracks. However, the problem of wild boar in Japan is seen as primarily a rural and agricultural one. In Germany, on the other hand, boar are very much an urban menace.

Kaigyokusai (Masatsugu), wild boar rooting, ivory netsuke, mid- to late 19th century.

Wild boar piglets decorate a car park in Hagi City, Japan.

A wild boar trio painted on the frontage of a timber store, Tokyo, Japan.

A boar family root through rubbish in a Berlin suburb.

Recently, Germany has seen a surge in its wild boar population. They have become a particular problem in Berlin, after the dismantling of the Berlin Wall in 1989 allowed them access once again to their historic range. This range now includes the city's suburbs, which, with their interconnecting green pathways, gardens, vegetable plots and orchards, provide a temptingly rich habitat. Enjoying a more abundant and more varied diet (given added spice by people who befriend and feed them), Berlin's boars, now reckoned to number up to 10,000, are living longer, maturing earlier and mating sooner. The trouble they cause is not limited to spoiling lawns, cemeteries and even football pitches as they root up the earth in search of grubs. In October 2012, four people, including a policeman, were injured when they were attacked by a 120-kilogram (265-lb) boar which had previously been hit by a car as it crossed a road (it has been estimated that boar are responsible for about 15 per cent of the city's traffic accidents).

Elsewhere in Germany, in Hamburg, in March 2010, seven boar invaded a U-Bahn metro station, where one was hit by a train. Power lines had to be switched off for over an hour while armed police hunted the rest of the herd. Meanwhile, another animal managed to smash through the toughened glass of a security window at the office of an IT consulting company, and caused several thousand euros' worth of damage as it rushed through the building, before being shot dead.

Volunteer huntsmen are permitted to cull the boar, which, in a town or city with many humans around, requires even more skill than shooting them in the wild. It also requires a thick skin: the bonus paid to the hunters for shooting piglets under fifteen weeks old has often made them the target of abuse. Scientists are exploring an alternative strategy of delivering contraceptives through pellets left in food troughs in the forest.

Yet not all relationships between boars and humans in Germany end badly. In summer 2009 a farmer, Heiko Cordt, helped to chase a herd of boar out of a friend's garden. In the confusion, one piglet got left behind, and Cordt hand-reared it, naming it 'Schnitzel'. It is now a member of a new herd, comprised of the farmer's five dogs – as well as being a star of the Internet.

In Britain, native wild boar became extinct several centuries ago, and the populations that have now established themselves in various parts of the country are the descendants of animals that have either escaped or been deliberately released from farms. A study in 1998 by MAFF (the Ministry of Agriculture, Fisheries and Food) confirmed the presence of two groups in southern England, one in Kent and East Sussex, the other in Dorset. A report in 2008 by DEFRA (the Department for Environment, Food and Rural Affairs – the successor to MAFF) identified a third sizeable population, in the Forest of Dean, close to the Welsh border. It also noted that boar were 'colonising areas

German farm owner Heiko Cordt with Schnitzel, his adopted wild boar.

around the fringes of Dartmoor and evidence of breeding in the wild has been recorded'.[9]

The DEFRA report estimated the total number of wild boar in England at 'fewer than 1,000', but the impossibility of accurate counting is reflected in its cautious statement that 'there may be in excess of 50 animals' in the Forest of Dean. In the 1990s escapees from a wild boar farm had settled in woodland near Ross-on-Wye, and then in 2004 a group of animals were illegally released near the village of Staunton above the Wye Valley. A photo of a sounder of about thirty animals in the nearby forest was published at the time, and by 2009 it was clear that the two groups had merged to form a sustainable breeding population.

In the DEFRA report, Joan Ruddock, Parliamentary Under Secretary of State, concluded: 'It is important that communities and land owners are allowed to decide the future of their wild boar populations based on their local situation. The Government's support will help them make the right decisions for where they live.' This marked a change in the status of boar under the law: as we have seen, as farmed animals, they had previously been

A field dug up by boar in the Forest of Dean.

included in the provisions of the Dangerous Wild Animals Act of 1976 and the Wildlife and Countryside Act of 1981, which makes it an offence 'to release, or to allow to escape into the wild, any animal that is not ordinarily resident in, and is not a regular visitor to Great Britain in a wild state.' Once the boar broke their boundaries, they became 'feral' (the DEFRA report was titled 'Feral Wild Boar: An Action Plan') and therefore, like wild deer or foxes, not the property of anyone. Responsibility for their management was shifted to the owners or managers of the land across which they roamed. The 'feral' label also removed boar from the protection the Wildlife and Countryside Act afforded to 'wild' animals, and legalized their hunting by farmers, landowners and private game shoots.

In the case of the Forest of Dean, responsibility for its wild boar population rested with the Forestry Commission, which began taking advice from interested parties. The Commission noted that the most obvious damage was to 'amenity grasslands' – play areas, sports pitches, caravan parks, gardens and golf courses – where the boar rooted in their search for food. There were also less easily quantifiable 'social impacts' – people terrified by the appearance of boar in their gardens or driveways, or afraid to ride their horses or walk their dogs in the woods. However, two-thirds (67 per cent) of local residents who answered a questionnaire in 2009/2010 said they were not concerned by the presence of free-living wild boar in the Forest of Dean. And a large majority (76 per cent) said they were either excited or interested when they saw a boar for themselves.

In 2009 the Commission concluded that the boar population in the Forest should be maintained, but reduced to about ninety animals from its presently estimated 150. This target was controversial: opponents argued that the smaller number would exhibit limited genetic variation due to the shrinking of the gene pool, resulting in poorer all-round health and greater susceptibility to disease. However, arguments became academic when it became clear that the cull targets were not going to be met: only 38 animals were removed in the financial year 2008/9. In defence, Kevin Stannard, the Forestry Commission's Deputy Surveyor, argued that it took up to four times longer to track down and shoot boar than deer, as their movements were so unpredictable. In subsequent years cull targets have increased, as has success in meeting them:

In March 2011 the population was estimated to have grown to between 300 and 350 animals. The cull target was left at 150 animals, even though logic dictated that the cull should have risen to 250. With a more focused effort the target of 150 animals was achieved by October 2011.[10]

The key word in this extract from the Forestry Commission's website is 'estimated'. Since the aim is to preserve a viable breeding population, the proportion of it that is removed is crucial – if too many are killed, the boar could be exterminated altogether. Yet counting boar in a forest is an incredibly difficult task. In 2010 the Commission – which had previously relied on the reports of its team of rangers to estimate boar numbers – undertook a thermal imaging survey, which revealed only sixteen animals. The following year a repeat exercise spotted no boar at all. (This, the Commission argued, was because they hid behind bracken.) In 2014, however, 835 boar were reported, and in 2015 the total jumped to 1,018, 'despite the cull of 361 animals' in the winter of 2014/15. (Of course, as well as the boar shot by Forestry Commission rangers, an unknown number are killed by poachers or on private land – there is no obligation for landowners to report such kills.)

The apparent dramatic increase in numbers was partly due to the more powerful thermal imaging cameras the Commission was using, but also to their reliance on a method known as 'distance sampling', pioneered by Steve Buckland, which allows the density of biological populations to be estimated according to the distance of an observed animal from a previously selected point or line.[11]

However, the design of the survey is crucial. The authors of *Distance Sampling* emphasize that the line transect must be random: 'A common mistake is to have lines follow established roads or corridors.' Yet critics point out that the Commission vehicles drove down existing forest tracks, which were in any case favoured locations for the boar, which like to root for food in the verges. They also charge the surveyors with failing to measure accurately the distance between observer and animal, a further key factor.

No one knows how many boar the Forest of Dean holds. The Forestry Commission justifies its culling policy by arguing that they are steadily increasing in numbers, and to do nothing would lead to serious social and environmental problems. 'They have no natural predators, so their population is growing unchecked,' says wildlife manager Ian Harvey.[12] According to Harvey,

> The problem is that wild boar numbers can increase very sharply over a short timescale. Indeed, biologists have noted that boar are the only large ungulate in the world with the population dynamics of rodents. We've seen litters in every month of the year and we've killed sows with up to 12 foetuses. You need to cull 70–80% of the population just to stand still.[13]

Harvey is also keen to deny that they are true wild boar: 'we describe them as feral wild boar . . . We strongly suspect that they are a mixture of larger East European wild boar and domestic pigs.'[14] In fact, most wild boar in Europe have some admixture of genes from domestic pigs so genetic purity is not particularly relevant. Harvey does not take into account the high mortality rate of newborn piglets (typically above 50 per cent[15]), from factors such as parasites, bacterial infections, hunger, cold or attack by other boar. Sounders of boar in the Forest do often include a large number of young animals, but these are likely to be the offspring of several sows, raised together and often co-suckled. The comparison with 'rodents' – a word with negative associations – seems also intended to stir up feeling against the boar and to justify an aggressive culling strategy.

As arguments and counter-arguments swing back and forth, the attitude of the public to wild boar is an important factor. On 7 April 2014, Greg Davies's wild boar farm near Maesteg in South

Wales was ransacked and a great deal of farming equipment stolen. Although the boar were not the thieves' primary target, they cut through the fences around their enclosure and several animals wandered loose on to the road. The raiders attacked some of them with hammers, or deliberately drove over them – two corpses were subsequently discovered in their van. The rest of the released animals – 38 in all – fled into the woods and surrounding countryside. Some were recaptured, or made their way back to the farm, but 24 remained at large.

The tabloids revelled in the incident's shock-horror value, warning the public not to approach the 'pack of stampeding wild boars', who were also described as 'tusked animals' and as 'dangerous giant pigs' – although a photograph of Greg Davies with his remaining herd showed them to be roughly the same size as farm pigs. Davies himself declared, 'They will attack if they smell blood.'[16] It fell to naturalist and broadcaster Iolo Williams to restore some perspective to the debate: 'They are very secretive, they are very shy and probably the first thing they'll do is they'll head for woodland cover. There's quite a bit of woodland in the Maesteg area – I'm pretty sure that's where people will find most of them.'[17]

Williams was proved right. After a prolonged search, which included setting camera traps near posts baited with peanut butter, jam and muesli, some of the escapees were filmed in their new habitat – evidence which proved crucial in convicting the Maesteg thieves of the additional crime of releasing a non-native species into the wild (they also admitted burglary and causing unnecessary suffering to an animal). It was the first time anyone had been prosecuted under this clause of the Wildlife and Countryside Act. Since then, some of the boar have been shot or poached, but several piglets appear to have survived the death of their mothers, and the presence of even younger animals shows that this new population has begun to breed.

Since their first appearance in the 1990s, in fact, wild-living boar have been a reliable source of scare stories in the British media. In 2008 locals were said to be angered by the refusal of former Beatle Sir Paul McCartney to allow the shooting of boar on his Peasmarsh estate in East Suffolk. 'The boar are doing huge damage. They are also dangerous if confronted . . . They are breeding like rabbits', one person complained, while the writer of the article blew facts to the winds with her assertion that these boar 'weigh up to 900 lbs . . . the same weight as a horse' – a British boar weighing 180 kilograms (about 400 lb) would be truly exceptional.[18]

In January 2015 boar received more unwelcome publicity when a Gloucester Old Spot pig belonging to Princess Anne was attacked and killed by a wild boar which broke into its pen at her Cotswold estate of Gatcombe Park. Sadly, the previous month had seen the first fatality from a road collision involving wild boar, when a motorist died after his car struck an animal on the M4 motorway in Wiltshire.

While exaggerated accounts of the boars' size and ferocity can be discounted, they have, on occasion, wounded dogs: vets in the Forest of Dean say they treat one or two boar-related injuries every year. Local resident Pepi Barrington describes one such incident: 'I'd just gone over a stile and all of a sudden this boar appeared from nowhere and shot past me. That's all I saw – this huge thing hurtling past with tusks. He went after two of the dogs – one of the Irish water spaniel bitches and the labrador. The spaniel turned round to look at me and the boar took a huge chunk out of her rear end. It got the labrador as well.' Both dogs have recovered, but Pepi now walks them with bells on their collars. She also points out that danger doesn't simply reside in the boar, but in the number of poachers armed with guns who have been attracted to the area. Little wonder that, in

her opinion, the boar are now harder to spot, as they have
retreated into the thickest areas of the forest and rarely venture
out during daylight.[19]

The Forestry Commission states that its aim, in culling wild
boar, is to 'limit the impacts of boar on those who live in, work
in or visit the Forest.'[20] To this end, they urge visitors not to feed
them, as this leads them to cluster round the Forest's many picnic
sites and cafés, where 'there have been instances of boar helping
themselves to visitors' . . . lunches.' However, they do not want
to eliminate the boar altogether, as they are a valuable part of the
estate – the Commission has contracts with local meat-processors
to supply a certain number of carcasses each season. It is difficult
to strike the right balance, especially when a true count is all but

unobtainable. An alternative to the Commission's present policy of quite severe culling has been proposed by Dave Slater, of local action group Friends of the Boar – that there should be no reduction of numbers within the Forest itself, but that boar which make their way outside its boundaries should be humanely shot. The idea is that the boar will regulate their own density within a particular habitat, with parties of them leaving when their numbers exceed what that habitat can sustain. A further viewpoint is provided by members of animal rights organizations, who vigorously oppose any killing at all.

Although most of the wild boar to be found in Britain descend from chance escapees from commercial farms, there have also been attempts to introduce them to certain areas in order to study their effect on local ecologies, sometimes as a prelude to a more general 'rewilding'. The Forestry Commission admits that 'at low densities' boar are likely to have a beneficial influence on the ecology of the Forest of Dean. Their characteristic rooting behaviour

A reassuringly peaceful encounter.

'break[s] up stable eco-systems and habitats allowing a greater diversity of plants to thrive, and thus support a greater range of insects.' However,

> repeated rooting of the same areas stops or slows re-colonisation so all that is left in some locations is bare mud. Equally, we know that several sites for rare or locally important butterfly colonies have been rooted by the boar and that is a potential cause for decline in butterfly numbers – although proving cause and effect is not that simple.[21]

In other words, it is fine for the boar to 'root' – as long as they don't overdo it.

In 2004 the Guisachan Wild Boar Project, in partnership with Trees for Life, released several wild boar inside fenced enclosures on the edge of Glen Affric National Nature Reserve in the Scottish Highlands. Here, overgrowth of bracken was shading out young pine saplings, and the aim of the project was to see if the boar could remedy the situation, since they will eat both bracken fronds (which are toxic to most animals) and the underground runners, or rhizomes, by which it spreads so quickly. The experiment was a success: the number of saplings was significantly higher in the area with boar than in the control area. The Guisachan project ended in 2007, but in 2009 Trees for Life released six boar donated by the Royal Zoological Society of Scotland's Wildlife Park in a fenced area of ancient birchwood on the Dundreggan Estate in Glen Moriston. Once again, their mission was to thin out the bracken, and they were hailed as 'eco-warriors' and as partners in a nation-wide plan to preserve and extend the once-great Caledonian Forest (of which only about 1 per cent now remains). 'Wild boar are outstanding ecological engineers,' said adviser Liz Balharry, who also coordinated the Guisachan project.[22]

Wild boar have been described as many things, but they are always characterized in the light of human concerns and priorities. Even when their natural behaviour is praised, humans limit the extent to which they are allowed to practise it. Although the Guisachan boar performed a valuable service in restricting the spread of bracken, once their numbers grew they also began to strip the bark from mature trees – an equally 'natural' way of feeding but one which was far less welcome.

Environmental activist and writer George Monbiot asks whether British people in fact have 'an unusually intense fear of wild animals', making them possibly 'the most zoophobic nation in Europe'. Monbiot points out that hardly any of the large land mammal species present in Britain after the last ice age have survived to the present day – now we have just the roe deer and the red deer and no big carnivores at all – while 'other countries as densely populated and industrialised as ours have managed to hang on to theirs'. Our bears, our wolves and our wild boar fell victim to a combination of early and extensive deforestation and the targeted attacks of human hunters.[23]

Monbiot was responding to a discussion on BBC Radio 4's *Farming Today* programme, in which Ralph Harmer of the Forestry Commission admitted that he did not have enough information to judge whether or not wild boar were damaging woodlands. Monbiot poured scorn on such ignorance, citing a Swedish thesis which showed that boar perform 'a number of critical ecological functions',[24] and directing his readers to

the Bialowieza forest in eastern Poland, where the flora of the woodland floor is fantastically diverse. In our woods a single species – bracken, male fern, bramble, wild garlic, bluebell or dog's mercury – often dominates. But the rooting and wallowing of Bialowieza's large population of boar prevents a monoculture from developing. To be in that forest in May, where dozens of species jostle in an explosion of colour, is to understand how much we're missing here.

Monbiot also criticized the programme for failing to mention that the boar is a native species. Instead, it was discussed 'as if it were an exotic invasive animal, such as the mink or the grey squirrel'.

The debate about wild boar in Britain is a continuing one, and connects with wider questions about rewilding and the reintroduction of top predators such as the lynx or the wolf. The factors that originally drove these animals to extinction are still present, and the hunters – licensed and illicit – are now armed with guns instead of spears. In addition, the scare headlines that proliferate

Sightseers flock to view boar in the Forest of Dean.

A roadside casualty in the Forest of Dean.

when there is even the barest rumour of a large wild animal in a neighbourhood show how unused we are, in both practical and imaginative terms, to accommodating creatures that are outside our immediate control. Meanwhile, the boar go on doing what they are well-practised at – surviving.

9 Encounters

In the summer of 1940 the American poet Robinson Jeffers was living with his family in Monterey County, California, in a granite house he had built himself. His poem 'The Stars Go Over the Lonely Ocean', partly drafted on the back of a letter of 23 July, and published in the December edition of the journal *Poetry*, describes his encounter with 'a black-maned wild boar' on the slopes of Mal Paso Mountain.[1] Jeffers was fervently opposed to U.S. involvement in the Second World War – a stance that he maintained even after Pearl Harbor – and he expressed his views through the boar, which refuses to bow to any ideologies and concentrates instead on what he finds beneath his snout as he ploughs up the turf, 'Fat grubs, slick beetles and sprouted acorns'. Although the boar acknowledges that the world is in a bad way, his remedy is simply to wait things out, lying up for 'Four or five centuries' if necessary. In the poem he is presented as a patriarchal figure, 'the old father of wild pigs' who has seen many generations come and go. The original animal Jeffers encountered did not have such an august history – his black mane indicates that he was actually a gone-wild Russian boar, one of several living on Mal Paso mountain. Nevertheless, the boar's gruff self-reliance, and his focus on simple survival, make him an effective spokesman for the poet's views. This is no fugitive creature, uncertain of its reception, and ready to bolt at the slightest hint of danger: the 'old monster' stands his ground, defying what he sees as political cant and asserting his trust in the enduring rhythms of the natural world. No fleeing into the woods for him – he is solidly present.

My own 'encounter' with wild boar turned out to be not an encounter at all. In January, in the Forest of Dean, I searched for signs of their presence with Dave Slater, of Friends of the Boar. We were not far from one of the roads crossing the forest, and car headlights frequently flashed through the trees. The ground was waterlogged after recent heavy rain, streaked with brown rivulets between tussocks of long grass and curled bracken.

Beside a small stand of conifers, where there was a dark, cave-like space beneath the branches, Dave and I kept perfectly still, trying to catch the slightest sound. It is in shelters like these that sows will give birth and stay for four or five days afterwards, suckling their newborn piglets and keeping them warm. Wild boar do

Neighbours meet in the Forest of Dean.

not breed all year round, but in January the first-time mothers typically produce their young, so they do not compete for resources with the older matriarchs, who have farrowed the previous autumn.

The forest was silent. However, signs that boar had been here recently were everywhere: piles of black droppings, hoofprints distinguished from those of deer by the characteristic dewclaw, rutted trackways where the animals had turned the soil over. Around one tree stump a large area had been excavated, leaving bare earth and mud – a great effort for the small reward of a few grubs or beetles.

The elusiveness of the boar – its preternatural sensitivity to danger – is an enduring traditional theme. 'Don't talk aloud about tomorrow's hunting', Japanese hunters used to warn each other, 'because the mice will go and tell the wild boar.'[2] A related

Forest crossing.

theme is the boar's apparent ability to survive against all the odds, as in the legend of Twrch Trwyth, who is never finally subdued, despite the best efforts of Arthur and his warriors. Today boar face the threat of modern weaponry, as well as a public profile distorted by myths of their monstrous size and unchained aggression. It is to be hoped that their ability to become invisible – or at least, very hard to spot – will continue to serve them well.

Dave and I gave up our search when it had become so dark we started seeing ghost animals among the trees.

Timeline of the Wild Boar

c. 16,500–14,000 BC	*c.* 9000 BC	4TH CENTURY BC	*c.* 37 BC
A wild boar is depicted in ochre and charcoal on the ceiling of a cave in Altamira, Spain	Bas-relief figures of boars are carved at the mountain sanctuary of Göbekli Tepe in present-day Turkey	The Greek writer Xenophon's *Cynegeticus* describes how to hunt boar; making of the Iron Age Witham shield, with its leather boar-figure	Varro's *De re rustica* describes the farming of boar for the table 

700–800	1198	*c.* 1350	1395
Carving of the Knocknagael Boar Stone, a Pictish symbol stone showing a wild boar	The English Assize of the Forest imposes harsh penalties on those who illegally hunt boar and other game	The exploits of the giant boar Twrch Trwyth are described in the *Mabinogion*	Accounts for The Queen's College, Oxford, show the purchase of a boar's head, most likely for the college's Boar's Head Feast

1611–12	1749	1961	1981
Peter Paul Rubens's painting of *The Calydonian Boar Hunt*	'Wild boar famine' in Hachinohe, Japan	Revival of the Boar's Head Feast at The Queen's College, Oxford	First wild boar farm opens in the UK

80–200	c. 98	c. 600	EARLY 7TH CENTURY
Making of the war-trumpet, the Deskford Carnyx	Tacitus describes the boar cult of the Aestii, a Baltic tribe	Making of the Gundestrup Cauldron, which depicts warriors wearing boar helmets	Creation of the Sutton Hoo treasure, which includes shoulder clasps decorated with paired golden boars

EARLY 15TH CENTURY	1483	1578	1608, 1611
Composition of *The Master of Game*, a popular hunting manual	Richard III is crowned king of England, and gives away many badges with his device of the white boar	Hans Hoffmann's portrait of *A Wild Boar Piglet*	English king James I releases imported wild boar in Windsor Great Park

1998	2004	2016
Report by the British government confirms the presence of free-living boar in the countryside	'Hogzilla', allegedly a massive wild boar, shot by Chris Griffin in Georgia, USA; Guisachan Wild Boar Project: boar are released in fenced enclosures in the Scottish Highlands to control overgrowth of bracken	Regional government in Tuscany, Italy, passes law extending hunting rights, in an effort to control the wild boar population

References

1 WHAT IS A WILD BOAR?

1 Brett Mizelle, *Pig* (London, 2011), pp. 12–25.
2 See Janet Backhouse, *The Luttrell Psalter*, The British Library (London, 1989), figs 16, 19.
3 Alain C. Frantz, Giovanna Massei and Terry Burke, 'Genetic Evidence for Past Hybridisation between Domestic Pigs and English Wild Boars', *Conservation Genetics*, XIII (2012), pp. 1355–64.
4 'Are the Free-living Wild Boar Pure-bred Wild Boar?', www.britishwildboar.org.uk, accessed 20 March 2016.

2 THE NATURAL BOAR

1 S. Saez-Royuela and J. I. Telleria, 'The Increased Population of the Wild Boar (*Sus scrofa* L.) in Europe', *Mammal Review*, XVI (1986), pp. 97–101.
2 Brett L. Walker, 'Commercial Growth and Environmental Change in Early-modern Japan: Hachinohe's Wild-boar Famine of 1749', in *JAPANimals: History and Culture in Japan's Animal Life*, ed. Gregory M. Pflugfelder and Brett L. Walker (Ann Arbor, MI, 2005), p. 182.
3 Jaroslav Červený et al., 'Magnetic Alignment in Warthogs *Phacochoerus africanus* and Wild Boars *Sus scrofa*', *Mammal Review*, XLVII (2016), pp. 1–5.
4 'The Boars that Wash their Own Food', www.bbc.co.uk, accessed 20 March 2016.

5 Pliny, *Natural History*, available at Loeb Classical Library (Cambridge, MA, 1947), book 8, chapter 78 (pp. 147–9).

6 Oppian, *Cynegetica*, available at Loeb Classical Library (Cambridge, MA, 1958), p. 145.

7 Ibid.

8 *On the Properties of Things*, John Trevisa's translation of Bartholomaeus Anglicus, *De proprietatibus rerum*, vol. II (Oxford, 1975), p. 1118 (spelling modernized).

9 *Les livres du roy Modus et de la royne Ratio*, ed. Gunnar Tilander, SATF (Paris, 1932), vol. I; quoted in John Cummins, *The Hound and the Hawk* (London, 1988), p. 109.

10 Edward Topsell, *The History of Four-footed Beasts, Serpents, and Insects* (London, 1658), pp. 537–46.

11 *Buffon's Natural History, From the French*, 10 vols (London, 1807), vol. V, pp. 278–302, online at www.gutenberg.org, accessed 7 March 2016.

12 Charles Darwin, *The Variation of Animals and Plants under Domestication* (London, 1868), vol. I, chapter 3.

3 THE LEGENDARY BOAR

1 Bacchylides, Fragment XVII (XVIII), in *Bacchylides: The Poems and Fragments*, trans. Sir Richard C. Jebb (Cambridge, 1905), p. 393; Ovid, *Metamorphoses*, Loeb Classical Library (Cambridge, MA, 1984), book 7, l. 433.

2 Plutarch, *Lives*, Loeb Classical Library (Cambridge, MA, 1914), vol. I, pp. 19–21.

3 Pausanias, *Description of Greece*, Loeb Classical Library (Cambridge, MA, 1935), book 8, chapter 46.

4 Ibid.

5 Homer, *The Odyssey*, trans. Robert Fagles (New York, 1996), book 19, l. 514 (p. 405).

6 'Grimnir's Sayings', in *The Poetic Edda*, ed. and trans. Carolyne Larrington (Oxford, 2014), verse 18 (p. 51).

7 Snorri Sturluson, *The Prose Edda*, trans. Jesse L. Byock (Harmondsworth, 2005), pp. 92, 93.

8 'The Song of Hyndla', in *The Poetic Edda*, ed. and trans. Larrington, stanza 5 (p. 246).

9 Ibid., stanza 45 (p. 251).

10 *The Mabinogion,* trans. Sioned Davies (Oxford, 2007), p. 209.

11 Ibid., p. 210.

12 Anne Ross, *Pagan Celtic Britain* [1967] (London, 1974), pp. 399–400.

13 Ibid., p. 400.

14 Thomas Blount, *Fragmenta antiquitatis: or, Ancient tenures of land, and jocular customs of manors* [1679], 3rd edn (London, 1815), pp. 557–60.

15 A. D. Mills, *A Dictionary of British Place-names*, revd edn (Oxford, 2003).

4 THE SYMBOLIC BOAR

1 Tacitus, *Germania*, Loeb Classical Library (Cambridge, MA, 1970), chapter 45 (pp. 207–9).

2 Polybius, *The Histories,* Loeb Classical Library (Cambridge, MA, 1970), pp. 343–5.

3 Anne Ross, *Pagan Celtic Britain* (London, 1974; first published 1967), p. 390.

4 See ibid., pp. 390–404.

5 *Beowulf*, ed. Fr. Klaeber, 3rd edn (Boston, MA, 1950), ll. 303–6 (my translation).

6 See Rupert Bruce-Mitford, *The Sutton Hoo Ship Burial: A Handbook*, 2nd edn (London, 1972).

7 Edward Topsell, *The History of Four-footed Beasts, Serpents, and Insects* (London, 1658), p. 523.

8 Thomas Heywood, *The First and Second Parts of King Edward iv*, ed. Richard Rowland (Manchester, 2005), p. 301 (part 2, scene 21).

9 See Karen Raber, 'The Tusked Hog: Richard iii's Boarish Identity', in *Animals and Early Modern Identity*, ed. Pia F. Cuneo (Farnham, 2014), p. 192.

10 Quoted ibid., p. 197.

11 See also v.6.74–5: 'The midwife wondered and the women cried / O Jesus bless us, he is born with teeth.'

12 E. A. Rees, *A Life of Guto'r Glyn* (Talybont, 2008),
   p. 211.

13 Glenn Foard and Anne Curry, *Bosworth 1485: A Battlefield
   Rediscovered* (Oxford, 2013), p. 125.

14 Bodleian MS Eng. misc. d. 227, ff. 139v–140r.

15 Geoffrey Chaucer, 'Sir Thopas', in *The Riverside Chaucer*, ed. Larry
   D. Benson, 3rd edn (Oxford, 1988), pp. 213–16.

16 Quoted in Raber, 'The Tusked Hog', p. 201.

17 Ibid.

18 Church Missionary Society, *Missionary Papers* (Oxford, 1828),
   no. lxv.

19 Gaia Pianigiani, 'They Feast on the Vines of Chianti, the Swine',
   New York Times (7 March 2016).

20 Ibid.

21 Ibid.

5 THE HUNTED BOAR

1 Xenophon, *Cynegeticus*, in *Scripta minora*, Loeb Classical Library
   (Cambridge, MA, 1984), 1.18 (p. 373), 12.1 (p. 433).

2 Plato, *The Laws*, trans. Trevor J. Saunders (Harmondsworth, 1970),
   7.824 (pp. 319–20).

3 Horace, *Satires, Epistles and Ars Poetica*, Loeb Classical Library
   (Cambridge, MA, 1970), *Satires*, 2.3.234–5 (p. 173).

4 Ibid., *Epistolae*, 1.6.56–61 (p. 291).

5 Pliny, *Letters and Panegyrics*, Loeb Classical Library, 2 vols
   (Cambridge, MA, 1969), book 1, letter 6 (vol. I, p. 17).

6 Marcus Aurelius, *Meditations*, trans. Robin Hard (Oxford, 2011),
   1.2 (p. 16).

7 *Asser's Life of King Alfred*, trans. Albert S. Cook (Boston, MA, 1906),
   pp. 20–21.

8 Ann E. Watkins, trans., *Aelfric's Colloquy*, available at www.
   kentarchaeology.ac/authors/016.pdf, accessed 20 March 2016.

9 Cecily Clark, ed., *The Peterborough Chronicle, 1070–1154*, 2nd edn
   (Oxford, 1970), p. 13.

10 See Charles R. Young, *The Royal Forests of Medieval England* (Leicester, 1979), pp. 60–73; David C. Douglas and George W. Greenaway, ed., *English Historical Documents*, vol. II: 1042–1189, 2nd edn (London, 1981), p. 453.

11 Edward, Second Duke of York, *The Master of Game*, ed. W. A. and F. Baillie-Grohman (London, 1904); *The Hunting Book by Gaston Phoebus*, trans. J. Peter Tallon (London, n.d.); *Turbervile's Book of Hunting, 1576* (Oxford, 1908).

12 Edward, *The Master of Game*, pp. 27–30.

13 Quoted in John Cummins, *The Hound and the Hawk* (London, 1988), p. 97.

14 Oppian, *Cynegetica*, trans. and ed. A. W. Moir, Loeb Classical Library (London, 1928), p. 145; Cummins, *The Hound and the Hawk*, p. 107.

15 *The Hunting Book by Gaston Phoebus*, pp. 88–9.

16 Edward, *The Master of Game*, p. 188 (appendix); Cummins, *The Hound and the Hawk*, p. 30.

17 Cummins, *The Hound and the Hawk*, p. 277, n. 15.

18 Quoted in J. E. Harting, *British Animals Extinct within Historic Times* (London, 1880), p. 104.

19 Ibid.

20 Ibid., p. 107.

21 Ibid., p. 108.

22 Quoted in Cummins, *The Hound and the Hawk*, p. 104.

23 See George Wingfield Digby, *The Devonshire Hunting Tapestries*, HMSO (London, 1971).

24 *Débat des héraulx d'armes* (Debate betwene the Heraldes), quoted in Cummins, *The Hound and the Hawk*, p. 97.

25 Quoted in Harting, *British Animals Extinct within Historic Times*, p. 85.

26 Ibid., p. 101.

27 Ibid.

28 *Letters to King James the Sixth from the Queen [and others], from the Originals in the Library of the Faculty of Advocates*, ed. A. Macdonald (Edinburgh, 1835), p. xxii.

29 John Aubrey, *The Natural History of Wiltshire*, ed. John Britton, Wiltshire Topographical Society (London, 1847), p. 59.

30 Gilbert White, *The Natural History of Selborne*, ed. Anne Secord (Oxford, 2013), letter 9 (p. 23).

31 Robert Baden-Powell, *Pig-sticking or Hog-hunting: A Complete Account for Sportsmen – and Others* (London, 1924).

32 Ibid., p. 20.

33 Ibid., p. 33.

34 Ibid., p. 51.

35 Ibid., pp. 57, 131.

36 Ibid., p. 205.

37 Robert Baden-Powell, *Lessons from the Varsity of Life* (London, 1933), chapter 3.

38 Rebecca English, 'Pippa, A Boar Hunt and Two Eligible Belgians: How Kate's Younger Sister Continues her Induction into the Upper Echelons of the Fabulously Wealthy', www.dailymail.co.uk, accessed 20 March 2016.

39 'The Mystery of Hogzilla Solved', abcnews.go.com, accessed 20 March 2016.

40 'Southeastern Trophy Hunters: News', www.imediaethics.org, accessed 20 March 2016.

41 'Alabama's Monster Pig Hoax, One Year Later', www.imediaethics. org, accessed 20 March 2016.

6 BOARS PORTRAYED

1 Rick Riordan, *Percy Jackson and the Titan's Curse* (New York, 2007), chapter 12.

2 Ovid, *Metamorphoses*, Loeb Classical Library, 2 vols (Cambridge, MA, 1984), book 8, ll. 281–99 (vol. I, pp. 425–7).

3 Ibid., ll. 340–44 (p. 431).

4 Ibid., ll. 414–24 (pp. 435–7).

5 Francis Haskell and Nicholas Penny, *Taste and the Antique: The Lure of Classical Sculpture, 1500–1900* (New Haven, CT, 1991), pp. 161–3; quotation on p. 161.

6 Tobias Smollett, *Travels through France and Italy*, ed. Frank Felsenstein (Oxford, 1979), letter xxviii.

7 Charles Godfrey Leland, *Legends of Florence, Collected from the People and Re-told*, 2nd edn (London, 1896).

8 Jean Hersholt, *The Complete Andersen* (New York, 1949). The full text is at 'The Metal Pig', www.andersen.sdu.dk, accessed 20 March 2016.

9 Ovid, *Metamorphoses*, book 10, ll. 503–739 (vol. II, pp. 101–17).

10 William Shakespeare, *Venus and Adonis*, in *The Complete Sonnets and Poems*, ed. Colin Burrow, *The Oxford Shakespeare* (Oxford, 2008), ll. 615–24 (p. 208).

11 Ibid., ll. 1111–16 (p. 232).

12 Geoffrey Chaucer, *Troilus and Criseyde*, in *The Riverside Chaucer*, ed. Larry D. Benson, 3rd edn (Oxford, 1988), pp. 471–585; quotation on p. 580 (book 5, l. 1519).

13 Gottfried von Strassburg, *Tristan*, trans. A. T. Hatto (Harmondsworth, 19760), pp. 219–20.

14 *Sir Gawain and the Green Knight*, trans. Keith Harrison, ed. Helen Cooper (Oxford, 2008).

15 Gaston Phoebus, *Livre de chasse*, ed. Gunnar Tilander, *Cynegetica* 2 (Karlshamn, 1971), chapter 53.

16 Anne Rooney, *Hunting in Middle English Literature* (Woodbridge, 1993), p. 85.

17 Neil Gaiman, *Neverwhere* (London, 1996), pp. 313–14.

18 Joe Lansdale, *The Boar* (San Francisco, CA, 2005).

19 Ibid., part 2, chapter 3.

20 Ibid., part 2, chapter 8.

21 Ibid., part 2, chapter 9.

22 Jonathan Watts, 'Japan in grip of blood-soaked cartoon film', *The Guardian* (5 November 1997), p. 16.

23 'Interview: Miyazaki Hayao on Mononoke-hime', trans. Toyama Ryoko, 18 March 2010.

24 Stijn Alsteens, 'Hans Hoffmann: A Wild Boar Piglet (*Sus Scrofa*)', in *Raphael to Renoir: Drawings from the Collection of Jean Bonna*, ed. Stijn Alsteens et al. (New York, 2009), p. 92.

25 Laurie Shannon, *The Accommodated Animal: Cosmopolity in Shakespearean Locales* (Chicago, IL, 2012), p. 101.

7 USEFUL BOARS

1 Varro, *De re rustica*, Loeb Classical Library (Cambridge, MA, 1934), 3.13.1 (p. 493).
2 Apicius, *L'art culinaire*, trans. Jacques André (Paris, 1974), 8.1 ('In Apro', pp. 87–91).
3 Petronius, *The Satyricon and the Fragments*, trans. John Sullivan (Harmondsworth, 1965), book 5, chapter 40 (pp. 54–5).
4 Pliny, *Natural History*, Loeb Classical Library (Cambridge, MA, 1947), book 8, chapter 78 (pp. 147–9).
5 René Goscinny, *L'Odyssée d'Astérix* (Asterix and the Black Gold, 1981), trans. Anthea Bell and Derek Hockridge (London, 1982).
6 René Goscinny and Albert Uderzo, *Astérix chez les Bretons* (Asterix in Britain, 1966), trans. Anthea Bell and Derek Hockridge (London, 1970).
7 René Goscinny and Albert Uderzo, *Astérix aux jeux olympiques* (Asterix at the Olympic Games, 1968), trans. Anthea Bell and Derek Hockridge (London, 1972).
8 'Quelle horreur! Asterix Surrenders to McDonald's', www.telegraph.co.uk, accessed 20 March 2016.
9 John Clubbe, *The History and Antiquities of the Ancient Villa of Wheatfield, in the County of Suffolk* (London, 1758), p. 30.
10 J. E. Harting, *British Animals Extinct within Historic Times* (London, 1880), pp. 95–6.
11 'Radioactive Wild Boar Roaming the Forests of Germany', www.telegraph.co.uk, accessed 14 July 2016.
12 See www.sillfield.co.uk, accessed 20 March 2016.
13 Harting, *British Animals Extinct within Historic Times*, pp. 110–11.
14 '8 Boar Bristle Brush Benefits', www.morroccomethod.com, accessed 20 March 2016.

15 Robert Baden-Powell, *Pig-sticking or Hog-hunting:
A Complete Account for Sportsmen – and Others* (London, 1924),
pp. 283–4.

16 Ruth Scurr, *John Aubrey: My Own Life* (London, 2015), p. 159.

8 BOARS AND HUMANS

1 Jeffrey Greene, *The Golden-bristled Boar: Last Ferocious Beast of the
Forest* (Charlottesville, VA, 2011), pp. 55–7.

2 Matsuo Bashō, *Genjuan no ki* (The Hut of the Phantom Dwelling),
translated in Haruo Shirane, ed., *Early Modern Japanese Literature:
An Anthology*, 1600–1900 (New York, 2013), p. 208.

3 Brett L. Walker, 'Commercial Growth and Environmental Change
in Early-modern Japan: Hachinohe's Wild-boar Famine of 1749',
in *JAPANimals: History and Culture in Japan's Animal Life*, ed. Gregory
M. Pflugfelder and Brett L. Walker (Ann Arbor, MI, 2005),
pp. 162–92.

4 John Knight, *Waiting for Wolves in Japan: An Anthropological Study
of People–wildlife Relations* (Oxford, 2003), p. 52.

5 Ibid., p. 54.

6 Ibid., p. 57.

7 Ibid., p. 58.

8 'Wild Boars and Deer are Overrunning Japan – and Women are
Out to Stop Them', http://qz.com/146514, accessed 20 March
2016.

9 DEFRA News Release, Ref. 48/08, 8 February 2008.

10 Forestry Commission, 'Feral Wild Boar in the Forest of Dean',
www.forestry.gov.uk, accessed 20 March 2016.

11 S. T. Buckland, D. R. Anderson, K. P. Burnham and J. L. Laake,
Distance Sampling: Estimating Abundance of Biological Populations
(London, 1993), pp. viii–ix.

12 *Forest of Dean and Wye Valley Review*, 21 June 2013.

13 Ben Hoare, 'Return of the Native', *BBC Wildlife*, XXXIII/3
(March 2013).

14 *Forest of Dean and Wye Valley Review*, 21 June 2013.

15 See András Náhlik and Gyula Sándor, 'Birth Rate and Offspring Survival in a Free-ranging Wild Boar *Sus scrofa* Population', *Wildlife Biology*, vol. IX, suppl. 3 (2003), pp. 37–42.

16 David Wilkes, 'Find the wild boar! 23 escape in Wales after burglar gang releases them from farm', *Daily Express* (28 April 2014).

17 Ibid.

18 Urmee Khan, 'Sir Paul McCartney Refuses to Cull Wild Boar on his Estate', *Daily Telegraph* (10 December 2008), www.telegraph.co.uk, accessed 20 March 2016.

19 Bella Bathurst, 'Here Comes Trouble: The Return of the Wild Boar to Britain', *The Observer* (4 March 2012), www.theguardian.com, accessed 20 March 2016.

20 Forestry Commission, 'Feral Wild Boar in the Forest of Dean'.

21 Ibid.

22 'Wild Boar: Our New Eco-warriors', *Herald Scotland* (26 November 2009).

23 George Monbiot, 'How the UK's Zoophobic Legacy Turned on Wild Boar', *The Guardian* (16 September 2011), www.theguardian.com, accessed 20 March 2016.

24 J. Welander, 'Spatial and Temporal Dynamics of a Disturbance Regime: Wild Boar (*Sus scrofa* L.) Rooting and its Effects on Plant Species Diversity', PhD thesis, Swedish University of Agricultural Sciences, Utgivningsort (2000).

9 ENCOUNTERS

1 Robinson Jeffers, 'The Stars Go Over the Lonely Ocean', in *Selected Poems*, ed. Colin Falck (Manchester, 1996).

2 John Knight, *Waiting for Wolves in Japan: An Anthropological Study of People–wildlife Relations* (Oxford, 2003), p. 70.

Select Bibliography

Albarella, U., K. Dobney, A. Ervynck and P. Rowley-Conwy, eds,
 Pigs and Humans: 10,000 Years of Interaction (Oxford, 2008)
Alsteens, Stijn, 'Hans Hoffmann: A Wild Boar Piglet (*Sus Scrofa*)',
 in *Raphael to Renoir: Drawings from the Collection of Jean Bonna*,
 ed. Stijn Alsteens et al. (New York, 2009), p. 92
Anderson, J. K., *Hunting in the Ancient World* (Berkeley, CA, 1985)
Baden-Powell, Robert, *Lessons from the Varsity of Life* (London, 1933)
—, *Pig-sticking or Hog-hunting: A Complete Account for Sportsmen –
 and Others* (London, 1924)
Barrios-Garcia, M. N., and S. A. Ballari, 'Impact of Wild Boar (*Sus
 scrofa*) in its Introduced and Native Range: A Review', *Biological
 Invasions*, XIV (2012), pp. 2283–300
Červený, Jaroslav, et al., 'Magnetic Alignment in Warthogs
 Phacochoerus africanus and Wild Boars *Sus scrofa*', *Mammal Review*,
 XLVII (2017), pp. 1–5
Cummins, John, *The Hound and the Hawk: The Art of Medieval Hunting*
 (London, 1988)
Dalix, Anne-Sophie, and Emmanuelle Vila, 'Wild Boar Hunting in the
 Eastern Mediterranean from the 2nd to the 1st millennium BC',
 in *Pigs and Humans: 10,000 Years of Interaction*, ed. Albarella et al.,
 (Oxford, 2008), pp. 359–72
Dutton, J. S., H. T. Clayton and S. M. Evans, 'The Social Aspects
 of Wild Boar in the Forest of Dean', unpublished report
 for the Forestry Commission by the University of
 Worcester (2015)

Edward, Second Duke of York, *The Master of Game* [*c*. 1406–13],
ed. W. A. and F. Baillie-Grohman (London, 1904)

Forestry Commission, 'Feral Wild Boar in the Forest of Dean',
www.forestry.gov.uk

Frantz, Alain C., Giovanna Massei, and Terry Burke, 'Genetic Evidence
for Past Hybridisation Between Domestic Pigs and English Wild
Boars', *Conservation Genetics*, XIII (2012), pp. 1355–64

Gaston Phoebus, *The Hunting Book by Gaston Phoebus*, trans. J. Peter
Tallon (London, n.d.)

Goulding, Martin, 'Possible Genetic Sources of Free-living Wild Boar
(*Sus scrofa*) in Southern England', *Mammal Review*, XXXI (2001),
pp. 245–8

—, *Wild Boar in Britain* (Stowmarket, 2003)

—, and Timothy J. Roper, 'Press Responses to the Presence of
Free-living Wild Boar (*Sus scrofa*) in Southern England',
Mammal Review, XXXII (2002), pp. 272–82

—, Timothy J. Roper, Graham C. Smith and Simon J. Baker, 'Presence
of Free-living *Sus scrofa* in Southern England', *Wildlife Biology*,
IX/3 (2003), pp. 15–20

Greene, Jeffrey, *The Golden-bristled Boar: Last Ferocious Beast of the
Forest* (Charlottesville, VA, 2011)

Harman, Derek, *British Wild Boar: The Story So Far*
(Brent Eleigh, 2013)

Harting, J. E., *British Animals Extinct Within Historic Times with Some
Account of British Wild White Cattle* (London, 1880)

Howells, O., and G. Edwards-Jones, 'A Feasibility Study of
Reintroducing Wild Boar *Sus scrofa* to Scotland: Are Existing
Woodlands Large Enough to Support Minimum Viable
Populations?', *Biological Conservation*, LXXXI/1–2 (1997),
pp. 77–89

Keuling, O., N. Stier and M. Roth, 'How Does Hunting Influence
Activity and Spatial Usage in Wild Boar *Sus scrofa* L.?', *European
Journal of Wildlife Research*, LIV (2008), pp. 729–37

Knight, John, *Waiting for Wolves in Japan: An Anthropological Study
of People–wildlife Relations* (Oxford, 2003)

Lemel, Jonas, Johan Truvé and Bo Söderberg, 'Variation in Ranging and Activity Behaviour of European Wild Boar *Sus scrofa* in Sweden', *Wildlife Biology*, IX/3 (2003), pp. 29–36

Morelle, K., T. Podgórski, C. Prévot, O. Keuling, F. Lehaire and P. Lejeune, 'Towards Understanding Wild Boar *Sus scrofa* Movement: A Synthetic Movement Ecology Approach', *Mammal Review*, XLV (2015), pp. 15–29

Náhlik, András, and Gyula Sándor, 'Birth Rate and Offspring Survival in a Free-ranging Wild Boar *Sus scrofa* Population', *Wildlife Biology*, IX/3 (2003), pp. 37–42

Raber, Karen, 'The Tusked Hog: Richard III's Boarish Identity', in *Animals and Early Modern Identity*, ed. Pia F. Cuneo (Farnham, 2014), pp. 191–207

Rooney, Anne, *Hunting in Middle English Literature* (Woodbridge, 1993)

Ross, Anne, *Pagan Celtic Britain* [1967] (London, 1974)

Saez-Royuela, S., and J. I. Telleria, 'The Increased Population of the Wild Boar (*Sus scrofa* I.) in Europe', *Mammal Review*, XVI (1986), pp. 97–101

Sir Gawain and the Green Knight, trans. Keith Harrison, ed. Helen Cooper (Oxford, 2008)

Sodeikat, Gunter, and Klaus Pohlmeyer, 'Escape Movements of Family Groups of Wild Boar *Sus scrofa* Influenced by Drive Hunts in Lower Saxony', *Wildlife Biology*, IX/3 (2003), pp. 43–9

Spitz, F., 'Current State of Wild Boar Biology', *Pig News and Information*, VII (1986), pp. 171–5

Sweeting, Steve, *Wild Boar: A British Perspective* (Leamington Spa, 2013)

Thiebaux, Marcelle, 'The Mouth of the Boar as a Symbol in Medieval Literature', *Romance Philology*, XXII (1969), pp. 281–99

Topsell, Edward, *The History of Four-footed Beasts, Serpents, and Insects* (London, 1658)

Walker, Brett L., 'Commercial Growth and Environmental Change in Early-modern Japan: Hachinohe's Wild-boar Famine of 1749', in *JAPANimals: History and Culture in Japan's Animal Life*, ed. Gregory M. Pflugfelder and Brett L. Walker (Ann Arbor, MI, 2005), pp. 162–92

Welander, J., 'Spatial and Temporal Dynamics of a Disturbance
    Regime: Wild Boar (*Sus scrofa* L.) Rooting and its Effects on Plant
    Species Diversity', PhD thesis, Swedish University of Agricultural
    Sciences, Utgivningsort (2000)
Woolley, Linda, *Medieval Life and Leisure in the Devonshire Hunting
    Tapestries* (London, 2003)

Associations and Websites

BRITISH WILD BOAR
www.britishwildboar.org.uk
Increases understanding of free-living wild boar in Britain.

FRIENDS OF THE BOAR
http://friendsoftheboar.blogspot.co.uk
An independent group based in the Forest of Dean, England, which supports the presence of boar in the UK, acts as their advocate in local and national media, and gives advice on how to live safely alongside them.

WILD BOAR
www.wild-boar.org.uk
Run by the Deer Initiative, this is a site covering 'feral' wild boar in England only; includes a tab to report sightings.

WILD PIG INFO
http://wildpiginfo.msstate.edu/index.html
Discusses the problem of feral pigs (including wild boar) in the USA.

Acknowledgements

My thanks to the staff of the Bodleian Library, the Alexander Library, the Radcliffe Science Library and the ZSL Library, especially Ann Sylph. Also to Chris Bailey of the Bowland Wild Boar Park, for talking to me about his boar, and to Michael Riordan, Archivist of The Queen's College, Oxford, for information about the college's Boar's Head Feast. I am extremely grateful to all the people who have generously made their photographs available on Wikimedia Commons. Special thanks to wildlife photographer David Slater of Friends of the Boar for showing me round the Forest of Dean, and for generously allowing me to reproduce some of his wonderful pictures.

Photo Acknowledgements

The author and the publishers wish to express their thanks to the below sources of illustrative material and/or permission to reproduce it.

The AMICA Library, Cleveland Museum of Art, Bequest of Noah L. Bulkin: p. 123; © The Trustees of the British Museum, London: pp. 24, 27, 35, 37, 38, 39, 40, 53 (top), 58, 60, 61, 96, 108, 118, 119, 138, 145, 149; www.thecityreview.com: p. 131; Fototeca Online A Comunismului Românesc, Photo no: #N155 (08.03.2009): p. 104; Trammell and Margaret Crow Collection of Asian Art, Dallas, Texas (photo by Joe Mabel): p. 32; Daderot: p. 137; Darjac: p. 101; Domski3: p. 155; Bernard Gagnon: p. 71; The J. Paul Getty Museum, Los Angeles: pp. 82, 84, 85, 112; BS Thurner Hof: pp. 92, 95; HTO: p. 106; Jza84: p. 49; Kabuto 7: p. 56; Collection Georges de Lastic: pp. 75, 98; Lomita: pp. 79, 100; Los Angeles County Museum of Art: pp. 129, 151, 152, 153; Valerie McGlinchey: p. 90; Momotarou2012: p. 154 (top); NASA (National Aeronautics and Space Administration): p. 147; The New York Public Library: pp. 36, 130; Andrzej Otrębski: p. 150; Portable Antiquities Scheme: pp. 64, 66; Purple128: p. 141; REX Shutterstock: pp. 50 (Photoservice Electa/Universal Images Group), 142 (De Agostini/G. Dagli Orti), 157 (Action Press); Helen Rickard: p. 81; Sailko: p. 107; Davids Samling: p. 127; Wolfgang Sauber: p. 111; Lowell Silverman: p. 148; © David J. Slater: pp. 6, 14, 17, 18, 21, 22, 158, 164, 165, 168, 169, 171, 172; Georg Slickers: pp. 109, 115; TT mk2: p. 154 (bottom); Kim Traynor: p. 53 (bottom); University of Toronto Wenceslaus Hollar Digital Collection: p. 87; Unukorno: p. 126; Vassil: p. 134;

The Walters Art Museum, Baltimore: pp. 12, 144; Neil Weightman: p. 78; Wellcome Library, London: pp. 16, 70; Dorothy Yamamoto: pp. 11, 44, 69, 143; Zoological Society of London: pp. 10, 28.

Index